Henri Troyat

Twayne's World Authors Series
French Literature

David O'Connell, Editor
University of Illinois

TWAS 616

Henri Troyat in 1981
Photograph by Nicholas Hewitt

Henri Troyat

By Nicholas Hewitt

University of Warwick

Twayne Publishers • Boston

*PQ 2639
R78
Z68
1984*

Henri Troyat

Nicholas Hewitt

Copyright © 1984 by G. K. Hall & Company
All Rights Reserved
Published by Twayne Publishers
A Division of G. K. Hall & Company
70 Lincoln Street
Boston, Massachusetts 02111

Book Production by Marne B. Sultz

Book Design by Barbara Anderson

**Library of Congress Cataloging
in Publication Data**

Hewitt, Nicholas.
    Henri Troyat.

    (Twayne's world authors series; TWAS 616.
French literature)
    Bibliography: p. 143
    Includes index.
    1. Troyat, Henri, 1911–   —Criticism and
interpretation. I. Title. II. Series.
PQ2639.R78Z68 1984   843'.912   83–12695
ISBN 0–8057–6458–5

For Kim and Rachel

Contents

About the Author

Nicholas Hewitt studied at the University of Hull, where he wrote his Ph.D. thesis on André Malraux, and at Harvard University, where he was a Kennedy Scholar from 1969–70. He has taught at the University of Hull and the University of Southampton and is currently lecturer in French studies at the University of Warwick. He is the author of a critical edition of Troyat's *Grandeur nature*, as well as numerous articles on Malraux, Céline, Sartre, and Queneau. He is currently preparing a book on Céline's work in the 1930s.

Preface

Henri Troyat was an immediately successful writer. His first novel was awarded a prestigious literary prize, and his books throughout the 1930s received solid critical recognition, culminating in the Prix Goncourt of 1938. After World War II that *succès d'estime* was turned into spectacular commercial success, with Troyat joining a select group of best-selling authors in France, with sales regularly over 100,000 copies. Paradoxically, this commercial profitability after the war has tended to erase the critical esteem in which his work is held.

There are at present no books devoted to Troyat, very few scholarly articles, and his name appears fleetingly in literary manuals covering the period and only in connection with his long novel cycles. His position in the literary history of France in the twentieth century is therefore by no means secure. There are several reasons for this neglect. Troyat works in a currently unfashionable mode, that of the realist psychological novel and the *roman-fleuve*, ("novel cycle"), both viewed as survivors from a previous literary era and lacking the textual complexity of more recent novels. Similarly, Troyat's success and prolific production have worked against him: the best-selling author cannot readily be accepted as a serious writer, worthy of analysis, and the sheer extent of Troyat's output, six novel cycles, sixteen psychological novels, and six biographies, has tended to overshadow and devalue the individual works.

The problem, of course, goes beyond mere literary snobbishness and Troyat's work presents real difficulties for the critic. He does not escape the role of best-selling author with total impunity, and some of his novels are seriously flawed by the introduction and exploitation of conventional stereotypes. Similarly, literary criticism is most easily turned to the study of innovation and departure from the norms, and adapts itself with difficulty to authors like Troyat who write comfortably within the parameters of literary convention. In other words, Troyat's novels can appear sufficiently self-explanatory to render the task of criticism redundant.

It is the aim of this study to remedy the critical neglect into which Troyat's work has fallen, by providing a description and analysis of all his major works and by attempting to situate them in the context of French literary history of the twentieth century. A detailed exploration of his work shows that neglect to be unjustified, and illuminates two major areas of significance, the intrinsic quality of some of the works themselves, particularly the *romans-fleuves* and the short stories, and Troyat's role as the representative in postwar French fiction of a nineteenth-century manner of narration which contrasts with the experimental novels of the 1950s and 1960s. In one sense, this role shows Troyat to be irremediably conservative in his approach to writing; more profoundly, his capability and popularity, culminating in his election to the French Academy, testifies to the continuing healthiness of traditional novel forms, too often ignored or assumed to be dead. Analysis of his realist fiction, therefore, yields important information on the literary base from which any experimentation must depart. Finally, Troyat, as the son of Russian émigré parents, introduces into French literature a unique blend of French and Russian cultural traditions which constitutes one of the riches of his work and goes a long way toward explaining its nineteenth-century quality.

In order to explore these features, a chronological approach is not the most helpful of methods. In the first place, biographical detail on Troyat is scarce and comes only from the author himself, and, apart from the early period of his life, Russia, and the flight to Paris, it is of little relevance to a study of his works. Second, Troyat's work does not develop in a unified linear manner, from his first novel in 1935 up to the present day. Rather, development and progression occur within the different genres which he uses, to the extent that the thematic structures and stylistic features of the novels, *romans-fleuves* and short stories appear to be rigorously compartmentalized. It is impossible to talk about the preoccupations of a long novel like *Tant que la terre durera (My Father's House)*, for example, in the same language which would be used to describe the short stories. Analysis of Troyat's work, therefore, is best carried out by genre, although this does not imply that a synthesis of the different modes of writing is impossible. Eventually, even the seemingly anomalous short stories may be integrated into a general view of the author, one which will tend to reinforce his position as a fundamentally conservative writer. That this conservatism is serious and important, and owes little to the trade of the popular novelist, is what the present work seeks to demonstrate.

My thanks are due to the University of Warwick for granting me a sabbatical leave in order to carry out the research for this volume, to M. Henri Troyat, for allowing me to discuss certain aspects of the book with him, to the staff of the Bibliothèque nationale and of the Library of the University of Aston in Birmingham, to Kathleen Wiggins and Sue Wallington of the Inter-Library Loan Section of the University of Warwick Library, and, finally, to my wife for her unfailing patience and support.

Nicholas Hewitt

University of Warwick

Chronology

1943 Jean-Daniel, son, born.

1944 Divorce. Becomes theater critic for *La Nef*.

1946 *Les Vivants, Pouchkine.*

1946–1948 Literary editor of *Cavalcade*.

1947 Visit to the United States. First volume of *Tant que la terre durera*.

1948 Second marriage.

1950 Completes *Tant que la terre durera*.

1951 *La Tête sur les épaules.*

1952 *La Neige en deuil*, wins the *Grand Prix Littéraire du Prince Rainier III de Monaco*.

1953 Begins publishing *Les Semailles et les moissons*.

1954 Journey to Central and South America.

1959 Elected to Académie Française.

1963 Mother dies.

1965 First volume of *Les Eygletière, Tolstoï*.

1967 Father dies.

1968 First volume of *Les Héritiers de l'avenir*.

1971 *Gogol.*

1973 *Anne Prédaille.*

1974 First volume of *Le Moscovite*.

1976 *Grimbosq.*

1977 *Catherine la Grande.*

1979 *Pierre le Grand.*

1980 *Viou.*

1981 *Le Pain de l'étranger, Alexandre Ier*.

1982 *Ivan le terrible.*

Chapter One
The Long Journey
From Moscow to Paris

The Frenchman Henri Troyat was born as the Russian Lev Tarassoff, in Moscow, on 1 November 1911. He was the youngest of three children, with a sister Olga, who subsequently studied ballet and emigrated to the United States, and a brother Alexander, who went on to become an engineer. His family were wealthy Moscow bourgeois: his father Aslan, like Michel Danoff in the novel cycle *Tant que la terre durera*, came from Armavir in the Caucassus, married Lydie Abessalomoff, the daughter of a doctor in Ekaterinoder, and managed the family drapery business with such success that, by the time of Troyat's birth, it was a nation-wide company with interests in banking and railways. Troyat's early years were therefore spent in the comfortable framework of the most privileged section of czarist society: the big house in Moscow, the servants, the coachman and the chauffeur, and, most important for the writer's later development, a Swiss governess who made him fluent in French even before his arrival in France. Of his early impressions of his parents, Troyat says little, except for noting the habitual seriousness of his father and remembering with pleasure the way in which his mother would tell him the old Russian folktales, a memory which surfaces clearly in his own short stories and plays a part in his ambition to be a "conteur d'histoires et créateur de mythes"[1] ("a storyteller and a creator of myths").

This quiet, luxurious, and solitary childhood was overturned by the Bolshevik Revolution of October 1917. As a prominent businessman, Troyat's father faced certain arrest if he remained in Moscow and he fled, almost immediately, to Kharkov in the south. By early 1918, however, his family's position had become completely untenable, and the mother led the children and the Swiss governess on that desperate journey through revolutionary Russia which Troyat transposes in the second volume of *Tant que la terre durera*. Reunited in Kharkov, the family then retreated to their estate in the Caucassus where they slipped back into the old luxurious way of life and waited for the Bolsheviks to be defeated in the civil war. The failure of the White Russian forces, however, and the permanent consolidation of Bolshevik power, threatened even the Tarassoffs' haven in the Caucassus and, in 1920, the family took the *Aphon*, the last émigré vessel out of the Crimea, for Constantinople. From there, they boarded another boat for Venice and then took the train to the growing Russian-exile community in Paris.

Troyat's parents found some difficulty in settling in France. On their arrival they had moved into a large apartment in the rue des Belles-Feuilles, in the prestigious Sixteenth Arrondissement, but left very quickly for the Russian community in Wiesbaden, where the French franc's superiority to the mark meant that their savings went further. Thus, Troyat, who had just become acclimatized to the Lycée Janson-de-Sailly in Paris, was uprooted and sent to the Lycée Français in Mainz. Postwar Germany, however, proved even less congenial than Paris and the parents quickly moved back to the French capital, settling this time in the boulevard Inkermann, in Neuilly, just opposite the Lycée Pasteur which Troyat attended until the end of his secondary education in 1930.

Troyat's early years in Paris were dominated by the experience of exile, both in his own sense of alienation and in his observations of the pathos of the Russian émigré community. In conversation with Maurice Chavardès, in *Un si long chemin* (Such a long journey), and in the third volume of *Tant que la terre durera*, he evokes the frustrating half-light in which the older generation of exiles lived. Unable to accept life in France, often incapable of speaking French, they lived in expectation of the imminent and inevitable fall of Bolshevism and their reinstatement among the czarist faithful. With the failure of the counterrevolution and the growing self-confidence of the Soviet regime, this expectation, clung to with more and more desperation, came increasingly to assume the quality of a pathetic self-delusion.[2]

Unable to be French, yet separated from their homeland, the exiles retreated into an increasingly meaningless self-reinforcing community, with its own language, religion, customs, and food. At the same time, the problems of the émigrés were multiplied by their financial vulnerability. Troyat recalls how his parents' savings, which they had carried with them in the form of cash and jewels, were quickly exhausted, and how their one last hope was frustrated when their considerable deposits in foreign bank accounts were frozen after the consolidation of the Soviet regime, despite a series of interminable lawsuits instigated by the father. Denied the private income on which they were relying, the family drifted down the slope of genteel poverty, marked out by the familiar milestones: the move to a smaller apartment, in Neuilly's avenue Sainte-Foy; the increasing difficulty in paying bills, especially Troyat's own lycée account; the inevitable failures of his father's investment in silent films and perfume manufacture; his mother's practical decision to set to work making hats for the more affluent members of the émigré community.

In this atmosphere of increasing poverty and faith in a return to Russia, Troyat's own position became ambiguous. His ability to speak French had already distinguished him from his parents by facilitating his integration into their new country; his attendance at a French lycée and his daily immersion in French culture accentuated that division. His parents and his older brother and sister still frequented predominantly Russian circles, but Troyat himself, as a member of the younger generation of exiles, came to regard this environment as strange and unreal in comparison with the French society in which he now lived. Thus, while Russia was, for his parents, a vital concrete memory, for Troyat it became subtly "le folklore de la patrie disparue"[3] ("the folklore of the lost homeland") and existed far more in its authors than in the shape of a real country in which one aspired to live.[4] This split between French and Russian influences is crucial to Troyat's later work. Not only does it guarantee a mingling of two powerful cultures in his writing, it is also responsible for a certain sense of isolation, never totally stifled,[5] which manifests itself in a stance of authorial detachment. In addition, the experience of exile during his adolescent years provides two major themes of his later fiction, the exploration of the relationship between Russia and France from the eighteenth century onward and an analysis of the phenomenon of exile itself, which constitutes one of the most pathetic and forceful elements of his postwar fiction.

Troyat's first years in France were marked by two processes: the increasing poverty and hardship of his family, and his assimilation into France both professionally and culturally. Troyat records, in his conversations with Chavardès and in his fictional transpositions of the experience, the desperate battle waged by his parents, culminating in the humiliation of the arrival of the bailiffs in the apartment in the avenue Sainte-Foy and the seizure and sale of the family furniture. This event, followed by the family's move to the place de la Nation, is avenged by Troyat in an heroic scene in his first novel, *Faux Jour* (Deceptive light). Nevertheless, if the family were falling into extreme poverty and increasing irrelevance as historical exiles, Troyat himself moved toward a successful position in French society, first as a civil servant and then as a respected writer.

His career at the lycée Pasteur reached its gratifying conclusion with his passing of the two parts of the Baccalauréat de Philosophie in 1929 and 1930. On leaving the lycée, he enrolled at the Sorbonne as a law student rather than as a student of literature, because the law course was only three years in length, instead of the usual four, and because the Licence de Droit, far more than the Licence ès Lettres, facilitated entry into the lucrative administrative professions. These financial considerations reflect a constant concern with his family's poverty, a concern which led him to look for work while he was studying and which saw him in the roles of a film extra, following in the footsteps of his favorite uncle, Constantine,[6] and commercial traveler in carbon paper and typewriter ribbons. Troyat was awarded his Licence de Droit in the summer of 1933 and decided to take the concours for the post of rédacteur in the prefecture of the Département de la Seine (Paris). In order to be accepted for the competition, however, it was necessary to become a French citizen, and Troyat broke his final links with a homeland he could barely remember by taking out naturalization papers. As a Frenchman, he passed the examination and was appointed to the Budget Department of the prefecture, a post he held until his resignation in 1942. It was just before he took up his post that he began his first novel, *Faux Jour*, the publication of which necessitated a change of name from Lev Tarassoff to Henri Troyat.

The period from Troyat's arrival in France to the publication of *Faux Jour* was also a time of general intellectual development, fostered by his lycée education, and, more specifically, of the development of a literary vocation. The picture tht he gives in *Un si long chemin* of a lonely child, living in a world of books and dedicating himself to a life of storytelling, recalls the account of Sartre's childhood in *Les Mots*. He recounts that his ambition to be a writer began at the age of ten, when he collaborated with an émigré friend, Volodia Bylinine, on a novel written in French, *Le Fils du Satrape*, of which only one chapter was completed.[7] At the same time, he made up stories and invented characters for his tin soldiers. This precocious literary production was continued in the first year of the lycée, when he wrote single-handed his own newspaper, which contained another unfinished novel, "L'Héroïque mission de Jean Manvel," and by the time he reached the third year, he had been inspired by his French teacher to concentrate on his own experiences and write a memoir of his flight from Russia.

In his last years at the lycée Pasteur, he came under the influence of the novelist and historian Auguste Bailly who introduced him to poetry and French classical theater. Under Bailly's relaxed guidance, Troyat experimented with verse, writing even his weekly exercises in poetry, and developed a profound knowledge of classical drama by writing pastiches of Racine. At the same time, by reading a novel of Bailly's, and noting the difference between the fictional events and the respectable personality of the author, he made the crucial discovery that experiences in novels are the work of the imagination and are not necessarily rooted in the real. In this period, Troyat's interests were by no means exclusively literary. With other pupils with literary aspirations he founded a review, *Fouillis*, which ran to six issues; but he was also fascinated by the theater and painting. The aspect of drama which most interested him was the way in which the mask served a protective function, a function to be found at the basis of many of his fictional characters. In painting he looked for a concrete experience ultimately denied the writer. These two abandoned ambitions are redeemed for Troyat in the art of the novelist who not only has to use the painter's skill at manipulating color, shapes, and decor, but must also use the dramatist's techniques of creating characters. The novelist therefore is "au fond . . . un peintre du dimanche et un acteur raté"[8] ("fundamentally a Sunday painter and a failed actor").

If the main influence of Troyat's lycée education was literary and artistic, however, he was also particularly grateful to his philosophy teacher, Dreyfus-Lefoyer, who introduced him to the works of Bergson and Freud. This led him to an enthusiastic interest in psychoanalysis and, while later following his law courses, he also attended lectures by Georges Dumas at the Hôpital Sainte-Anne. From this period dates Troyat's first short story, of which he comments: "Mon héros de *La Clef de voûte* aurait pu être un de ses malades!"[9] ("The hero of "La Clef de voûte" could have been one of his patients") and in this grounding in psychology and in his later fictional interest in what Marcel Arland terms "monstres,"[10] he resembles closely Georges Simenon's pride that *L'Homme qui regardait les trains* figured on psychology syllabuses.

Throughout his years at the lycée, Troyat was building up a knowledge of two literary traditions, that of his native Russia and that of his adoptive France. He records that, as an adolescent, even though Russian was the language of the household, his reading knowledge of the language was poor. To remedy this defect, therefore, he began, with enormous effort, reading *War and Peace* aloud. After this introduction to Russian literature through Tolstoy, he continued with Pushkin, Gogol's *Dead Souls*, Dostoevski, and Chekhov's short stories. At the same time, he gained a basic grounding in the classic nineteenth-century novels of Balzac, Stendhal, Flaubert, and Victor Hugo. From adolescence onward, therefore, the French and Russian traditions merge together in Troyat, forming "une seule coulée, puissante et large"[11] ("one single powerful broad current"). The formal techniques of this current of fiction were explored when, in the last years at the lycée, he rejected poetry and returned to prose writing. In order to develop a style in French, he used the same procedure as that for learning Russian, and so read aloud the novels of Flaubert and Stendhal and the memoirs of Saint-Simon. In addition to this, he worked on broadening his vocabulary by systematically going through the Larousse dictionary, a task which left him with a lifelong love of such books, and began putting his newly discovered techniques and skills into practice by writing carefully worked short stories.

It is from 1930 that Troyat's professional literary career may be said to date. In the years 1925–30 his uncle, Nikita Balieff, visited Paris with his own theater company, the Chauve-Souris, which presented sketches in Russian with some considerable success. Toward the end of these visits he had the idea of translating some of these sketches into French and chose his nephew as adaptor. As an experiment in itself it was unsuccessful: Troyat reckoned without the Russian inability to pronounce the French *u* sound, which rendered his translations unintelligible and comic when performed, and his libretto for a comic opera based on Chekhov's *The Double Base* was so badly acted that it was disastrously received. Nevertheless, it provided him with experience of the theater, to be used as material in novels like *Grandeur nature (One Minus Two)* and the Lioubov episodes in *Tant que la terre durera*, as technique in his own plays, *Sébastien* and *Les Vivants* (The living), and as mastery of dialogue in all the fictional works.

It was at the same time as the adaptation of *The Double Base* that Troyat wrote his first piece of extended fiction, the novella "La Clef de voûte" (The keystone), published in book form with its companion, "M. Citrine," only in 1937. One of his best friends at the time was Michelle Maurois, the daughter of the novelist and biographer, who showed the story to her father. He commended Troyat on the work and advised him to submit it for publication, either to Jean Paulhan, editor of the *Nouvelle Revue Française*, or to Robert de Saint-Jean at the *Revue Hebdomadaire*. Paulhan's reaction was courteous and encouraging, but in the end he returned the manuscript. Saint-Jean, however, accepted the work enthusiastically, complimented Troyat on his talent, and advised him to write a novel as soon as possible. It was this advice that he was about to take up as, a newly created Frenchman, he prepared to start his duties in the prefecture of the Seine.

The Working Novelist

The period in Troyat's life between his naturalization as a French citizen in 1933 and the liberation of France in 1944 sees a rapid mastery of four literary genres: the short novel, the novella and short story, the biography, and the *roman-fleuve*, a mastery which earned him critical respect and wide popularity at a very young age. At the same time, after the troubled events of his childhood and the poverty of his adolescence, he enters a peaceful, calm existence, in which his private life is carefully shielded and where historical incursions are kept largely at bay. With his assumption of a literary pseudonym, the life of Henri Troyat becomes the life of his books.

One of the results of his French citizenship was French military service, which he did in the 61st Régiment d'artillerie hippomobile, at Metz, from October 1933 to October 1935, postponing his entry into the civil service. It was thus as a soldier that he saw his first novel published, and as a soldier he wrote and published his second novel, *Le Vivier* (The fish-tank). Troyat had sent the manuscript of

Faux Jour to his mentor, Robert de Saint-Jean, who had advised him to send it to the publishing house of Plon, who were subsequently to publish most of his work until the mid-1950s. Plon accepted the novel, but insisted that it be published under a French name, to avoid confusion with Russian émigré memoirs. Troyat came naturally as a gallicization of Tarassoff; Henri was chosen simply by chance. The novel met with considerable success when it was published in 1935: Troyat's youthfulness, though little else, made comparison with Raymond Radiguet inevitable, and, in spite of the relatively minor populist elements in the novel, it was awarded the Prix populiste by the jury of Jules Romains, Georges Duhamel, Robert Kemp, André Thérive, Gabriel Marcel, and Frédéric Lefèvre, a group toward which Troyat was to gravitate in his later literary inclinations.

Le Vivier, published later that year, was partly written while its author was in charge of the regiment's radio workshop in Metz. It attracted more mixed reviews than *Faux Jour*, but nevertheless served to consolidate Troyat's position as a well-known young writer. In particular, the reviewer for the *Revue Hebdomadaire*, Jean Davray, was enthusiastic, and introduced Troyat to Claude Mauriac. The two got on well and, together with Michelle Maurois and Troyat's friend Jean Bassou, they formed a literary "club" in which they discussed each others' manuscripts as well as more general literary issues. This "club" served to reflect Troyat's fundamentally conservative taste in modern literature: he remembers "nos auteurs favoris: Mauriac, Maurois, Montherlant, Colette, Gide, Giono, Martin du Gard, Valéry."[12]

In October 1935 Troyat, finally released from military service, was able to take up his post in the prefecture. Like his post in Metz, his functions were not totally time consuming and allowed him ample time for writing. It was in this period that he published his third novel, *Grandeur nature*, in 1936, contributed to various newspapers the short stories later collected in *La Fosse commune* (The common grave), of 1939, prepared the volume containing "La Clef de voûte" and "M. Citrine," and worked on his most difficult novel to date, *L'Araigne* (The spider), which won the Prix Goncourt in 1938. With this prize, Troyat, at the age of twenty-seven, reinforced his reputation as a literary prodigy; at the same time, like all *Goncourt* winners, he became a famous and relatively wealthy writer. Troyat's reaction to this fame, however, was characteristically cautious: he declined to give up his safe post in the prefecture for the insecurity of the life of the professional writer. Although much of this caution is explained by the world situation and the Munich crisis, and amply justified by events, it highlights a major feature of Troyat's writing, a deep-seated apprehension and insecurity, present from one end to the other of *Un si long chemin* and at the base of his fiction.

The completion of *L'Araigne* and the award of the *Goncourt* nevertheless mark a break in Troyat's life and career. At the beginning of 1939 he was married and moved to an apartment in the Twelfth Arrondissement. Professionally, he temporarily abandoned fiction in order to concentrate on a completely new project, a biography of Dostoevski. Troyat explains this departure by various factors, insisting particularly that a change in genre made following the success of *L'Araigne* much easier. More important, the biography, necessitating detailed research in the Bibliothèque Tourgenieff, constitutes a departure from the format of the earlier novels and allows him to experiment with more extended fiction based upon historical documentation. In other words, *Dostoievski* opens the way to *Tant que la terre durera*.

The biography was published as Belgium fell in June 1940. Troyat, who had taken the "attaché d'Intendance" examination while doing military service, was mobilized and sent to the Service de ravitaillement in Tulle, where Boris Danoff meets Elizabeth Mazalaigue in the last volume of *Les Semailles et les moissons (The Seed and the Fruit)*. It was here, on 23 June, five days after the original broadcast, that Troyat heard de Gaulle's appeal for resistance, and reflected on the defeat of his chosen country: "La décision des armes ne consacre pas le triomphe de l'Allemagne sur la France, mais le triomphe de l'esprit de violence, de racisme, de nationalisme aveugle sur l'esprit de tolérance et de raison"[13] ("The military decision did not represent the triumph of Germany over France, but the triumph of the spirit of violence, racism and blind nationalism over the spirit of tolerance and reason"). Demobilized after the Armistice, Troyat returned to Paris, resuming his duties at the prefecture and renewing contact with Claude Mauriac. His post, however, immediately came under threat from the Occupation law banning anyone from public service who was not "Français de naissance"[14] ("French by birth"). Troyat, as a White Russian, managed to evade dismissal, but was furiously indignant at the treatment suffered by the real targets of the law, the French Jews. Although the gloom of the Occupation is rarely dealt with directly by Troyat, except in *La Rencontre (The Encounter)*, the frustration and the misery are evoked indirectly in *La Lumière des justes (The Light of the Just)* or *Le Moscovite* which deal with the occupation of Paris and Moscow during the Napoleonic Wars.

For a writer who has the reputation of rapid and copious literary production, Troyat published little during the Occupation: the three novellas in *Le Jugement de Dieu* (The judgment of God), in 1941, and the novel, *Le Mort saisit le vif* (The dead man siezes the living), in 1942. Thereafter, nothing appeared until *Le Signe du taureau* (The sign of Taurus) in 1945. In part, this lack of publication is explicable by the introduction of paper rationing in 1942, which reserved supplies for books by authors with pro-German sympathies. More specifically, however, Troyat's silence in the years 1942–45 is due to his single-minded concentration on his first *roman-fleuve*, *Tant que la terre durera*, which, initially planned as an antidote to the gloom of the Occupation, became a long-term project spanning ten years. If neither the success of *L'Araigne* nor the law on nationality could induce Troyat to abandon his job at the prefecture, the demands of his long novel led to his resignation in 1942. Encouraged by François Mauriac, to whom he had shown the manuscript in 1943, Troyat embarked upon the career of a full-time professional writer from which he was never again to deviate.

The Best-Seller

The years immediately following Liberation were a period of intense activity and experimentation for Troyat. His private life was marked by the breakdown of his marriage and by his remarriage in 1948. His second wife, Guite, whose husband had been killed by the Germans at Chamonix, became an indispensable source of information about provincial France in the same period as that covered by *Tant que la terre durera*, and acted as a valuable collaborator in Troyat's literary work.

Professionally, while writing the final volumes of *Tant que la terre durera* and preparing the biography of Pushkin which appeared in 1946, Troyat entered a new field of journalism. He worked briefly as theater critic for the review *La Nef* and, together with the novelist Maurice Druon, founded a new weekly magazine, *Cavalcade*, edited by the former head of the left-wing weekly of the 1930s, *Marianne*,

Jean-José Andrieu. Troyat's role in the new publication was that of literary editor, concerned with commissioning and selecting manuscripts, and also, briefly, that of film critic, a post he relinquished because of his significant dislike of judging a work of art. Ironically, the theater critic appointed by Troyat, Jacques Gautier, had as his first task the review of his employer's play, *Les Vivants,* in 1946. Gautier disliked it and wrote a damning article which Troyat loyally printed. Eventually, however, the magazine suffered the same fate as countless other ephemeral publications of the post-Liberation period and was wound up in 1948. Troyat's last article in it was an extract from his travel book on the United States, *La Case de l'oncle Sam* (Uncle Sam's cabin).

If Troyat's constant interest in the theater emerged in his brief role as theater critic for *La Nef,* it reached its zenith in the production of two of his plays, *Les Vivants,* and *Sébastien,* performed in 1949. Apart from his early adaptations from the Russian, *Les Vivants* was Troyat's first full-scale theatrical experiment: a stylized, allegorical treatment of the Occupation through a Renaissance plague, a subject which predates that of Camus's *La Peste.* While disagreeing with his reviewer Jacques Gautier and maintaining that the play had many admirable qualities, Troyat discovered one central fact about the theatrical experience which ultimately prevented him from fully exploiting the genre: the fact that, as rehearsals progress, the play escapes from the author and becomes the property of the director. Thus, while he made a further attempt with *Sébastien,* a comedy for the Théâtre des Bouffes-Parisiens, he still recognized the advantage of fiction over drama, that the former does not depend on outside forces for its performance and interpretation. Thereafter, he produced only a television adaptation of *Le Vivier, Madam d'Arches a dit peut-être,* Troyat's own favorite, and a skillful radio play, *L'Assassinat d'Alexandre II* (The assassination of Alexander II).

La Case de l'oncle Sam was the result of a journey made by Troyat in 1947 to the United States where he had been invited to teach as visiting professor at Mills College, in Oakland, California. The invitation provided him with the opportunity to see his sister Olga again, now running a ballet school in New York, and to measure the size and significance of the United States as he traveled across the country by train and by car. While disconcerted by the modernity of the civilization, Troyat nevertheless appreciated the real kindness of the people. At Mills, he was particularly pleased to meet Darius and Madeleine Milhaud, who taught there and who introduced him to San Francisco. *La Case de l'oncle Sam* is the first of three attempts at documentary writing: from his journey to Central and South America in 1954 came *De Gratte-ciel en cocotier* (From sky-scraper to palm tree) and, in 1960, he explored the Renault plant at Boulogne-Billancourt to write *Naissance d'une Dauphine,* (The birth of a "Dauphine"). It is not a genre at which Troyat excells: the "ton amusé"[15] ("amused tone") which he adopts tends to create a Jacques Tati-like persona, in irremediable conflict with modern life, which serves to mask the reality and becomes flagrantly frivolous when confronted with any serious issues. Paradoxically, for a realist novelist, Troyat is more successful when working with his imagination or when resurrecting a biography from archival documents than when dealing with contemporary reality.

The experimentation of the post-Liberation period, therefore, produces no new lasting interest on Troyat's part. Journalism, theater, and reportage give way to the constant preoccupations of biography and fiction, and for the rest of his career it is this framework which dominates his production. Thus, in the thirty years following *Tant que la terre durera,* he writes five *romans-fleuves,* nine short novels, a collection of short stories, four literary biographies, and two historical ones. It is this massive literary production which has raised Troyat to the small group of writers who regularly sell more than 100,000 copies of their works and whom Gilbert Ganne calls "Messieurs les best-sellers,"[16] a group which includes Georges Simenon, Jean Lartéguy, Françoise Sagan, and Hervé Bazin.

In addition to this popular success, Troyat's postwar work has received serious critical recognition. His novel *La Neige en deuil (The Mountain),* of 1952, won the Grand Prix Littéraire du Prince Rainier III de Monaco, following the previous year's award to Julien Green. His journey to Monte Carlo for the prize-giving ceremony allowed him to meet one of the "club's" favorite authors of the 1930s, Colette, who was a member of the jury, on which Troyat himself was later to serve. Finally, in 1959, at the unusually early age of forty-eight, he was elected, unopposed, to the Académie Française, on the death of the exotic adventure-novelist Claude Farrère.[17] This election, which saw a repetition of the ceremonies surrounding the award of the Prix Goncourt in 1938, consecrated Troyat's position in French society and literary life. As he himself recognized in *Un si long chemin,* the academician who paid a courtesy call on President de Gaulle had come a long way from the Moscow town house on Skaterny Street and the seizure and sale in Neuilly's avenue Sainte-Foy. At the same time, Troyat entered a group with whom he had close affinities as a writer: Maurois and Mauriac who were his sponsors at the reception ceremony, and friends such as Maurice Druon, Pierre Gaxotte, Joseph Kessel, and the film-director René Clair. Those writers honored by the Academy in recent years have been precisely those "storytellers and creators of myths" whom Troyat from his earliest years strove to emulate. In addition, the formal work of the Academy, the complication of its dictionary, was the logical culmination of Troyat's careful initiation into French style through reading the pages of Larousse.

The final, long period of Troyat's career merely accentuates features present throughout: concentration on his profession as "un artisan de la plume,"[18] ("an artisan of the pen") working regular hours each day, followed by almost automatic popular success and recognition, with a corresponding retreat into his private life, in his apartment in the rue Bonaparte or his farmhouse in the Loiret, and a resolute detachment from political and social currents. In spite of the superficial importance of his early biography, an understanding of his work is only to be achieved by an exploration of its literary qualities and the literary and intellectual background against which it is set. In this "homme d'ombre, de travail, de solitude,"[19] ("self-effacing, hard-working, lonely man"), it is the "travail" which is the key element.

The "Romancier Classique"

The originality of Troyat in French literary history lies initially in the way in which he is the sole authentic exponent of two major cultural traditions, the French and the Russian. As R.-M. Albérès, who compares his position to that of the Anglophile American Henry James, writes of him: "L'oeuvre de Troyat est . . . une double chronique, une chronique à deux choeurs (et à deux coeurs), une symphonie pour deux orchestres"[20] ("Troyat's work forms a double chronicle, a chronicle sung by two choirs [and by two hearts], a symphony for two orchestras"). At the same time, that originality should not disguise the fact that, in many important respects, he is highly selective in his exploitation of the two cultures, that his professional training lies in a careful reading of the major nineteenth-century French and Russian novels, with his subsequent emphasis in his own work on their features of narrative, individual psychology of character, and exploration, or at least establishment, of social context. In this way, Troyat occupies a traditionalist, noninnovative position in the history of twentieth-century French literature, a position clearly indicated by the literary preferences of the "club" in the 1930s, and rewarded by popular success in terms of sales and the accolades meted out by the literary establishment. His own entry into the Academy, joining such figures as Maurois, Mauriac, Jules Romains, and Maurice Druon, serves as an important reminder of the persistence and success of the traditional genres of psychological novel, *roman-fleuve* and biography, often masked by the publicity devoted to changes in literary fashion.

Valéry's dictum that it is no longer possible to write novels beginning with the words "La Marquise sortit à cinq heures"[21] is an exaggeratedly categorical comment on an intensely complex relationship in literary history between the traditional and the innovative, and ignores the fact that, while a literary vanguard must constantly reappraise and expand existing modes, a literary mainstream may continue to exploit those modes and, indeed, remain the necessary precondition for experimentation. The case of Troyat, however, raises two questions: not merely his aloofness from successive literary movements, but also the problem of the benefits and limitations of a career spent writing in one particular tradition.

Toward the end of his conversations with Chavardès, Troyat characteristically lays claim to be considered only as a working writer.[22] For this reason, he denies the importance of his private life by not keeping a diary, and, like Roger Martin du Gard, refuses to elevate the writer to a position of guru by giving lectures or writing articles. This attitude toward his profession contains also the dominant features of his work as a whole: it is resolutely nonintellectual, almost anti-intellectual, rejecting the manipulation of abstract ideas and, indeed, finding the practice dangerous; for this reason, Troyat is led to refuse conscious experimentation in fiction, precisely because it subjects the art of the storyteller to preestablished intellectual confines: "Il faut se méfier, à mon avis, des romans sur rails"[23] ("In my opinion one should distrust novels which run on rails"); finally, the refusal of intellectuality and the rejection of a doctrinaire role for the novelist lead him to a vigorously held nonpolitical stance, in which his own innate liberalism combines with his belief in the autonomy of his fictional characters.

Troyat's relatively narrow range of interests, therefore, and his insistence on the professional nature of the writer, tends to remove him from what have been commonly considered the main currents of literary innovation and experimentation from World War I onward. His interest in dreams, for example, derives from a somewhat superficial nineteenth-century tradition of Bohemianism, and owes little to the work of Proust, the writings of the "fantaisiste" group around Max Jacob and Francis Carco, or the noisy explorations of the unconscious by the surrealists. While this does not need to appear as a criticism in itself (and most serious writers of the 1920s were at pains to keep their distance from Breton and his collaborators), it nevertheless denies Troyat the very real possibilities of creative renovation exploited by later debtors to surrealism, such as Francis Ponge, Julien Gracq, and Raymond Queneau, particularly in the field of literary language.

In the same way, Troyat's concentration, in his short psychological novels of the 1930s, on narrow claustrophobic relationships from which broader intellectual issues are excluded, denies him access to one of the most successful areas of the French novel in the interwar years, the return to high tragedy through fictional metaphysical speculation. In this context, Troyat's selective exploitation of the atmospheric and narrative possibilities of Russian literature is significant in the way it excludes a major Russian influence on twentieth-century French literary and intellectual life, the tradition of philosophical anxiety. His comments on Russian authors in the long final section of *Sainte Russie, Souvenirs et réflexions* (Holy Russia, memories and reflections), and his full-length studies of Dostoevski, Pushkin, Lermontov, Tolstoy, and Gogol, have radically different preocupations from Gide's Vieux-Colombier lectures on Dostoevski or the writings of one of the most influential Russian émigrés living in Paris, Leo Shestov, on the Pascalian element in Dostoevski's thought and the modern sense of absurdity in Tolstoy's *The Death of Ivan Ilitch* and *The Master and his Servant*. Yet it was Gide's Dostoeveski and Shestov's metaphysical writings, in which Dostoeveski, the later Tolstoy, and Pascal combine with Kierkegaard and Nietzsche to constitute the type of modern man confronted with an inexplicable destiny, which influenced and set the tone for a whole generation of metaphysical novels, from Malraux's *Les Conquérants* to Sartre's *La Nausée,* through Céline's *Voyage au bout de la nuit,* Drieu la Rochelle's *Le Feu follet,* Louis Guilloux's *Le Sang noir* and Bernanos's *Journal d'un curé de campagne.*[24]

Troyat refuses to embark in this direction, which leads necessarily to a subordination of character to abstract representation: the resemblance of his isolated, self-enclosed protagonists to those of François Mauriac or Julien Green, to whom they are often compared, is misleading since they lack the implicit Catholic dimension which informs *Thérèse Desqueyroux* or *Adrienne Mesurat.*[25] Nor is Troyat unconsious of such a refusal: his novels consistently demonstrate a deep distrust of the weakening of basic human values in the face of intellectual concerns. Gérard Fonsèque, in *L'Ariagne,* dies because, like the hero of *Crime and Punishment,* he embraces principles of intellectual superiority which he is emotionally unable to sustain; the salvation of the protagonist of *Le Mort saisit le vif,* of 1942, lies in his final rejection of the alien persona of the acerbic pessimistic novelist, who bears a striking resemblance to Céline, in favor of his own unintellectual way of life; finally, *La Tête sur les épaules* (Levelheaded), of 1951, must be read, despite Troyat's denials, as an attack on the irresponsible pretensions of Sartrean existentialism to govern its followers' way of life.

The anti-intellectualism of Troyat's fiction is reinforced by its apolitical qualities, which further serve to distinguish it from the major preoccupations of French novel writing during the 1930s and the 1940s. One brief mention of the *crise* ("depression"), in *Grandeur nature,* together with the setting of *Judith Madrier* in the period of the Phony War, constitute Troyat's sole concession to contemporary political events in his interwar fiction, which remains silent on the rise of French fascism, the Front Populaire, the Spanish Civil War, and the threat of a general European conflict. Although he does return to these historical elements, in the later volumes of *Les Semailles et les moissons,* of the 1950s, they are then comfortably in the past and, even so, are present more as oblique allusions rather than as any direct significance for the Mazalaigue family in their symbolic haven in the French Alps. The novels are therefore far removed from that body of fiction of the 1930s in which politics becomes a powerful motive force: the left-wing novels of Guilloux and Paul Nizan, the rediscovery of the political epic by Malraux, the anarchist provincialism of Giono, the right-wing search for strength and purpose in the works of Drieu la Rochelle and Robert Brasillach, the obsessive fear of a second war which dominates the final volumes of Roger Martin du Gard's *Les Thibault*.

Such isolationism is justified by Troyat on the grounds that "Je n'ai pas la tripe partisane. Mon caractère me porte à voir en toute chose le pour et le contre"[26] ("I am not instinctively partisan. My character makes me see the for and against in everything"), and that the imposition on a novel of a preconceived political viewpoint would inhibit the freedom of his characters and color the impartiality with which he presents their stances and actions. Thus, in *Tant que la terre durera* he is able to follow with equal objectivity the careers of the czarist officer Akim, and of his brother, the Bolshevik Nicolas. A removal of the contempoary political context, however, has certain direct consequences for the type of fiction that is produced. In the psychological novels it leads Troyat to seek a setting, either in the financially cocooned world of the bourgeoisie, as in *Le Vivier* or *L'Araigne,* or in the marginal areas of bourgeois society, as in *Faux Jour* or *Grandeur nature,* whose populism is of a very different order from that of Eugène Dabit or Henri Poulaille. In the *romans-fleuves,* however, while social and political issues are evoked, they are handled at an historical remove which serves to neutralize their direct political effect. Troyat's authentic populist writing is contained, not in *Faux Jour,* but in the evocation of pre-World War I Paris in the early volumes of *Les Semaillles et les moissons.* Finally, in all the novels historical change and the pretension to implement it are shown as ultimately futile and the direct enemy of the destiny of the human individual, which is happiness.

The most poignant of Troyat's novels is *L'Eléphant blanc* (The white elephant), the final volume of the ironically named *Les Héritiers de l'avenir* (The inheritors of the future), in which aging revolutionaries who have devoted their lives to the overthrow of the czar are washed up on the shores of exile in Paris and finally realize how much they have lost in the exercise of politics and the pursuit of power.

The refusal of intellectuality, which leads Troyat to steer his novels away from metaphysical and political fiction, leads him, finally, to reject any notion of literary self-consciousness which makes an end of the work of art itself: "Trop de cervelle et pas assez de tripes, on meurt vite de cette maladie-là"[27] ("Too much intelligence, and not enough emotion, that disease can kill you quickly"). Troyat's fictional tradition is different from that which begins with symbolism and modernism and serves as the basis for postwar French experimental novels of the type produced by Alain Robbe-Grillet, Marguerite Duras, and Michel Butor, in which the one unifying element of the so-called "nouveau roman" is the belief that, in Jean Ricardou's dictum, "Ainsi un roman est-il pour nous moins l'écriture d'une aventure que l'aventure d'une écriture"[28] ("For us, therefore, a novel is less the narration of an adventure than the adventure of a narration"). To a certain extent, Troyat may be seen to have overstated his position: he admits to a considerable interest in the language of his novels, and, in a work like *Le Mort saisit le vif,* touches on a more modern fictional technique by making the narrator's letter the text of the authentic novel he was unable to write. Nevertheless, he would depart strongly from an assertion like that of Raymond Queneau that the reader of a novel should not be insulted by having his task made too easy,[29] and would place traditional elements such as character and plot far above self-reflexiveness in literary language. In *La Case de l'oncle Sam* he recounts a visit to a Chinese theater in San Francisco, and confesses his disappointment: "J'admets que le théâtre chinois est parvenu à la pointe du raffinement et que la convention a tué la vie. Cet art quintessencié, traditionnel, minutieux, ne vise pas à évoquer l'existence quotidienne, mais à la transposer en symboles durables"[30] ("I admit that the Chinese theater has reached a high point of refinement and that convention has destroyed its life. This quintessential, traditional, scrupulous art form is not attempting to evoke day-to-day life, but to transpose it into durable symbols"). Troyat's constant ambition in his fiction is precisely this evocation of daily life and not in the direction of the exploration of signs.

    In his aloofness from the literary trends of abstraction, *engagement,* and literary self-awareness, Troyat occupies an unfashionable position in twentieth-century French literature. Holding firmly to a realist fictional tradition, which so many writers have sought to expand or overthrow, he has concentrated on the basic art of storytelling with a limited number of themes: claustrophobia, domination and dependency, the conflict between dream and reality, in the short novels, which place him in the same literary family as the de-Catholicized Mauriac and Green, and Simenon and Hervé Bazin; in the *romans-fleuves* these themes are replaced by general reflections on Franco-Russian relations and the futility of history, as well as the powerful consideration of the phenomenon of exile, but at no time does Troyat break out of the traditionalist mold. The only exception to this pattern is constituted by the short stories, which he refers to revealingly as a form of relaxation from his more serious works.[31] It is these stories—which owe much to the influence of Gogol—which represent the most exciting part of Troyat's literary production, precisely because they are a release from the realist world into a disturbing fantasy land in which the language itself assumes a greater importance.

In spite of the contrasts between the short stories and the other fiction, however, it would be unjust to condemn Troyat for remaining within the realist tradition. Literary history has tended to devote a disproportionate attention to innovation, while neglecting the fruitful exploitation of continuing modes of writing. Similarly, pressure upon a writer to innovate when he is at ease in the fictional forms he has chosen can produce unfortunate consequences: Troyat's experiments with changes of tenses in a stream-of-consciousness manner in *Une Extrême amitié* (An extreme friendship), for example, mar rather than enhance the novel. At the same time, however, the unchanging working of a preestablished tradition presents problems, particularly for prolific authors such as Troyat or Simenon. In the first place, it is questionable to what extent novelty or originality can be sustained in a long series of novels following a similar format before evolution gives way to repetition: in a sense, the confines of any one particular novel form dictate a finite number of original narratives. In this situation, the novelist becomes faced with a choice between repeating a well-liked story in a different context, in which case superficial details of decor become all-important, or, as in the case of Anouilh's postwar drama, introducing technical innovation to disguise the repetition. Troyat is not immune from either of these dangers. His short fiction does not evolve greatly in the problems it treats: Etienne Martin, in *La Tête sur les épaules,* suffers from the same adolescent egoism as his counterpart in *L'Araigne* fourteen years earlier; the triumph of the dream life in *Le Front dans les nuages* (*Head in the Clouds,* 1976), is an exact echo of the apotheosis of Guillaume at the end of *Faux Jour.* Attempts to vary the location, as in *La Neige en deuil* with its setting in the Alps, or to change the time scale and return to eighteenth-century Russia, as in *Grimbosq* and *Le Prisonnier No. 1* (Prisoner no. 1), do not totally conceal the fact that the same thematic area is being exploited. Similarly, the recurrence of certain character types can owe more to the unconscious

use of literary stereotype than to a continuing originality: in his
fascination with the figure of the cynical irresistible lover, Troyat
produces a startlingly fresh character in the person of Kisiakoff, in
Tant que la terre durera, only to provide a pale conventional echo in
Christian Walter in *Tendre et violente Elizabeth.*

Clearly, these difficulties concern not merely the general problems
of literary renewal in an established context, but the specific features
of the commercial best-seller, in which the continued marketing of
proven formulas is an important factor. In this context, the shift of
location in some of Troyat's later novels to the Champs-Elysées/
Etoile area, and his description of the upper bourgeoisie in *Les
Eygletière* coincide with a popular vicarious interest in the lives of
the rich. In this way, Troyat's use of the *roman-fleuve* may be seen
to derive from certain constant features in popular extended fiction:
Cecil Saint-Laurent, in conversation with Gilbert Ganne, points out
that the continuing success of the *roman-fleuve* in France after World
War II owes as much to the popularity of English-language novels
like *Gone with the Wind* and *Forever Amber* as it does to the prestigious
tradition of extended Russian fiction or the work of Romain Rolland,
Jules Romains, Georges Duhamel, and Roger Martin du Gard.[32]
In other words, an examination of Troyat, particularly his contri-
butions to the popular and commercially successful genres of the
roman-fleuve and biography, cannot avoid taking into account those
features which have made him one of the ten best-selling authors
of the postwar period, but have often denied him serious critical
consideration. It is highly significant that the *Nouvelle Revue Française,* which reviewed his early novels and novellas with considerable
enthusiasm, gives no discussion of his postwar work.

Troyat's "long journey" takes him from Russia to the Académie
Française, but also from the realm of the respectable nineteenth-
century novel to its more dubious popular twentieth-century counterpart. Only a close analysis of the individual works will show how
his use of the genres of short novel, *roman-fleuve,* and short story
enables him to transcend the popular constraints of his adopted
forms and to produce an important contribution to French fictional
development.

Chapter Two
Novels 1935–45

Troyat's postwar literary reputation has been based almost exclusively on his long novel cycles, from *Tant que la terre durera* onward, to the extent that broad synthetic works of criticism, such as those by Pierre de Boisdeffre, R.-M. Albérès, and Louis Chaigne,[1] mention little else. Nevertheless, it was his work in the genre of the short psychological novel throughout the 1930s which established him as a well-known writer, which won him his literary prizes, and which constituted an apprenticeship which allowed him to develop in other areas after the war.

These novels of the 1930s and the war years all follow the same tight format. Like the novels of Mauriac and Simenon, they are all of medium length, never exceeding 250 pages, and all manipulate a small cast of characters in an indeterminate setting in which the interior life and psychological geography take precedence over specific external location and decor. The provincial setting of *Le Vivier*, for example, is used purely to signify the retreat from the real world and is in a different category from Mauriac's use of the *landes* or Giono's symbolism of Provence. Similarly, the fact that the apartment in *L'Araigne* looks out on the place des Vosges is of minimal importance compared with Céline's evocation of the First Arrondissement in *Mort à crédit* or the use of Montmartre made by Francis Carco and Pierre Mac Orlan. Within this psychological context, Troyat's novels explore a limited number of themes: the ambiguous attraction and repulsion exerted by a claustrophobic situation, often centered on the family; a struggle for power within that situation, with an oscillation between extreme dominance and abnormal passivity; a recurrent meditation on the authenticity of the individual, in which the role of intellectual pretension is prominent and where the symbolism of the actor and the mask is constantly employed. Finally, Troyat keeps returning to the initial problem posed by *Faux Jour*, the conflict between the relative merits of the reality principle and an attempt at escape and transcendence through the dreamworld, a conflict which becomes that between social responsibility and irresponsibility.

In their thematic range, as in their length and format, these short novels, in spite of some inevitable overlapping, form a well-defined and distinct category in Troyat's work, which demarcates them from the *romans-fleuves* and the short stories and novellas, both of which introduce preoccupations and writing techniques not to be found in the short fiction. Similarly, even within the context of Troyat's continuing exploitation of the genre after the war, the novels of the first period, from *Faux Jour* (1935) to *Le Signe du taureau* (1945), form a separate group. The short novels of the second period, from *La Tête sur les épaules* (1951) onward, show a much more sporadic interest in the genre, now facing heavy competition from the *romans-fleuves* and the biographies, and exhibit an often uneasy balance between repetition of established themes and attempts at innovation. Troyat's fiction of the 1930s and the war years, on the other hand, takes his thematic range and technical expertise to a point of fulfillment before the problem of limitation poses any real threat.

Faux Jour

Although J. S. Wood's comment that "Troyat's first book was hailed by all the major critics as the literary event of the year"[2] is needlessly exaggerated, critical reaction to *Faux Jour* was none the less favorable, summed up by Jean Vaudal's conclusion that it was "un début bien remarquable"[3] ("a quite remarkable début"). The novel, narrated by the protagonist's son Jean, begins with a family Christmas party in his childhood. He describes the luxurious setting of a bourgeois home, but concentrates on the magical figure cut by his father, Guillaume, as he acts as master of ceremonies, lighting the candles on the Christmas tree, distributing presents, performing conjuring-tricks. This scene, in which the father appears as "le génie même de la forêt natale,"[4] ("the very spirit of the forest"), able to transform any banal reality into a dream, echoes, often ironically, but finally in triumph, throughout the novel. After this prologue, the narrator recounts how his mother had died when he was eight and how he was sent to live with his aunt. Guillaume, suddenly liberated from the constraints of family, travels on business to America, a voyage which in itself encapsulates the element of dream of riches together with financial disaster which characterizes his subsequent career, and returns only to disrupt the aunt's way of life to such an extent that father and son set off together in pursuit of the father's dreams. Thereafter, moving to ever cheaper apartments, to ever seedier hotels, Jean becomes the powerless observer and chronicler of his father's chimerical schemes to make money and his easy love affairs, eventually coming to hate Guillaume and to despise him for the wrong he has done to the family. As the novel follows its inexorable course, father and son end up among the card players and dreamers of the Parisian bars, the only remotely populist element in the book, who exert such a strong influence on Jean that he too, through tiredness, enters the fantastic life of the imagination. It is too late to bring about a real reconciliation with Guillaume, however: his hypochondria, for once, masks a real illness, and he dies in a sordid hotel room. His son, however, has learned by now that appearances are illusory and that his father in life and poverty-stricken death constitute a curious triumph. At the very end of the novel, watching over Guillaume's body, he reflects: "Vraiment, au terme d'une vie dédiée aux belles actions et comblée de réussites miraculeuses, mon père n'aurait pas eu un autre visage" ("Truly, at the end of a life dedicated to fine actions and rewarded with miraculous successes, my father would not have had a different face," 159).

The novel, which follows a straightforward linear development from episode to episode, is centered on the character of the father, Guillaume, who is a combination of several literary types. In his laxness and his faith in a beneficent future, he owes much to Dickens's Micawber; as a childlike inventor of ever more improbable schemes, such as the manufacture and marketing of yogurt from a minute office, he resembles the hero of H. G. Wells's *Tono Bungay,* George Ponderevo; as a mythomaniac who embarrasses his family, he is related to Dostoevski's General Yepanchin in *The Idiot;* finally, on a small scale, Troyat is attempting the same kind of portrait as that of Raymond Pasquier in Duhamel's *Le Notaire du Havre* (1933), in which the narrator is, similarly, the protagonist's son. In this way, Guillaume's irresponsibility takes several forms. His constant belief in the succession of failed money-making projects underlines a curious blend of dynamic inventiveness and fatalistic acceptance that their success depends upon higher authority: in other words, he is a gambler. At the same time, his mythomania is built upon a faith in language as a value in itself, rather than as a representative of concrete reality. The very act of speech creates the dreamworld in which he lives: the sign has more substance than the object it signifies. One example of this concerns the period immediately following Guillaume's return from America, in which the text is punctuated with English vocabulary. This culminates in the paradox by which the pathetic, sleazy yogurt-office is saved and transfigured by "la magique inscription: *Private*" on the door ("the magic inscription: *Private,*" 54).

This flight into language and refusal of the reality behind it constitute one of the major components of Guillaume's irresponsibility. It is for this reason that Troyat employs an entire pattern of theatrical imagery to underline the schism between stylized over-conscious rhetoric and the real situation, a pattern he is to repeat in subsequent novels. Thus, faced with Guillaume's unjustified confidence in the yogurt venture, Jean asks himself, "N'était-ce pas une comédie qu'il nous jouait pour nous berner?" ("Wasn't he acting a part in order to dupe us?" 67), and, of his father's empty-headed mistress, Gisèle Bennet (an Anglicization of "benêt"), he refers to her "personnage de gamine distraite qu'elle croyait adroite de jouer" ("the part of an absent-minded young girl which she thought it clever to act," 70). The problem becomes amplified toward the end of Guillaume's short life, when he has lost all confidence as an individual and is merely the sum of his past roles or lies: in this way, his personality has all but disappeared, and the narrator asks himself anxiously: "Comme ces vieux acteurs rendus à l'oisiveté, ne pouvait-il se retrouver lui-même hors des rôles qu'il avait joués?" ("like those old retired actors, was he unable to find himself outside of the parts he had played?" 141). More serious than the destruction of the personality, however, is the way in which the fascination with language can lead Guillaume to the most dangerous social irresponsibility. After the failure of the yogurt scheme, he announces to a horrified but skeptical Jean that he will recoup their fortune by writing a 300-page racist pamphlet, warning of an invasion of Europe from the East, in the tradition of the *Action Française* and the more radical anti-Semitic right.

Significantly, it is through language that Guillaume's language-based dreams are punctured, precisely because there is no substance to them and, in a world deprived of all but linguistic reality, one confident verbal assertion is worth any other. Hence, his lyrical description of the yogurt sales is destroyed simply by the contradiction of his partner, Fisquet, "Ce n'est pas vrai!" ("it's not true!" 65), and his stories to his later companion, Babillot, are again deflated by a direct verbal challenge. In other words, linguistic fantasy is vulnerable, not so much to reality, which it can normally dominate, as the baron de Clappique does at the end of Malraux's *La Condition humaine,* but to other language: and in this respect, Troyat looks forward to a crucial scene in Céline's *Mort à crédit* (1936), in which the narrator's father sees his grand but untrue stories of his travels destroyed by a neighbor marking the letters *MENTEUR* ("liar") on his window.

With this vulnerability of language, Guillaume's mythomania encounters severe dangers, indicated by his social decline, illness, and death. His last days spent playing "belotte" in cafés with his equally mythomaniac and hypochondriac friends, Babillot and Trollette, contain all the features of his failure: an exaggerated preoccupation with the self, a retreat into an endlessly repeated, artificial ritual in the game of cards, an element explored further with the game of patience in *Le Vivier,* an inability to escape, all combine with the dangerous effects upon his son to create what appears as the archetypal portrait of the "raté," a figure who recurs in the person of Antoine Vautier, in *Grandeur nature.* Nevertheless, although all the elements of failure are present, there is a certain grandeur and heroism in Guillaume's rejection of the servitude implied by modern life—"Tu oses me lier à la galère des salariés!" ("You dare to tie me to the slave galley of work!" 104), he reproaches his second mistress, Hortense—and in his magical talent for turning *réalité* ("reality") into *rêve* ("dream").

The ambiguity is compounded by the role of Jean, who is present in the novel both as son and as narrator. It is probably by no means coincidental that the father should be called Guillaume: he stands in the same relation to his son as does Wilhelm Tell to his and, like Tell's son, Jean experiences a mixture of love, admiration, fear, and revulsion at a series of experiments of which he is the most conspicuous victim. This mixture of emotions is responsible for a feature of the narrative which Jean Vaudal regrets but which is amply justified by the scope of the novel as a whole: the way in which the narration becomes much harsher toward Guillaume after the affectionate nature of the first fifty pages.[5] In fact, Jean's reactions and growing bitterness are quite explicable on several counts:

the magical attraction exerted by Guillaume is most effective in relation to events of the past, such as the Christmas party; continued firsthand experience of his irresponsibility and its repetition quite naturally leads to disillusionment after a short time. This disillusionment coincides with the particular sensitivity felt by Jean as an adolescent toward any form of peculiarity: hence, his hatred for Guillaume begins with the realization that "Il nous avait déclassés" ("he had made social outcasts of us," 124), and this adolescent fear of social abnormality and shame is reinforced by sheer nostalgia for the comfort and respectability of his aunt's house, a nostalgia which grows deeper with each descent into poverty. Thus, throughout the middle part of the novel, Troyat enters into what will become his familiar territory: a struggle for survival among members of one family, which culminates in "une sorte d'espionnage du père par le fils, une lutte" ("a sort of spying on the father by the son, a struggle," 143).

At the same time, however, this later antagonism disguises the constant fact, which only becomes clear at the end of the novel, that Jean has inherited his father's qualities. Although he fights as hard as possible in favor of the reality principle and against the world of dreams, he discovers in himself the same flaw which characterizes Guillaume, a lack of willpower. Hence, when he surrenders to the collective mythomania of his father and his companions, he recognizes "cette désertion de ma volonté" ("this desertion of my willpower," 135). Yet this negative character trait becomes part of a more positive discovery of the true significance of his father's role: the ability of the dreamlife to transform and transcend reality, in spite of what appear as defeats in the eyes of the world. In this way, the novel constitutes a negative *Bildungsroman*, in which Jean is assimilated, not into the real way of life of bourgeois society, but into the brotherhood of marginals and dreamers. For this reason, the present he receives at the Christmas party is significant. It is a "boîte de prestidigitateur" ("a conjuring kit," 9), which the father immediately borrows in order to entertain and entrance the guests, a present which looks forward to Jean's ultimate role as narrator of his father's story in which he becomes a manipulator of words and a creator of magic himself. It is this assumption of the part of the writer by Jean which constitutes the real revenge of the "saisie et vente" in the novel and in Troyat's own past.

The dichotomy between "rêve" and "réalité" is conveyed by the title of the novel itself, which not only signifies the unreal world in which the action takes place, in the reflected light of the Christmas tree candles, but also poses the ambiguity of Guillaume, that most of his actions appear in a false light in which their true value is hidden or deformed. More specifically, however, the title has aesthetic connotations to do with the lighting techniques of realist painting before the impressionist revolution. As Céline remarks, in his prologue to *Guignol's Band,* "Le Jazz a renversé la valse, l'Impressionisme a tué le 'faux-jour,' vous écrirez 'télégraphique' ou vous écrirez plus du tout!"[6] ("Jazz killed off the waltz, impressionism killed artificial light, you'll adopt a telegraphic style or you'll give up writing"), a comment which emphasizes the fact that, while Troyat recognizes the richness of the term "faux jour," he nevertheless still retains its realist technique in the face of radical innovation. This specific painting terminology seems to underline the fact that Guillaume's project and the world in which he moves are essentially aesthetic. In this context, the abundance of theater images convey not merely the inauthenticity of Guillaume, but also his artificiality: the stage benefits from the same artificial lighting as does the realist painting. In the same way, in this artistic world, the fact that the son becomes the narrator of the novel is highly appropriate. The novel therefore constitutes a complex piece of writing in which the thematic structure, which is centered on artificiality, becomes a mirror for the novel form itself.

It is a complexity which the subsequent novels rarely attain. After *Faux Jour,* the ambiguity of the dreamlife which recognizes both its richness and destructiveness disappears in favor of a less equivocal condemnation of the inauthenticity and irresponsibility it entails. In this way, the imagery of the actor and the theater comes to convey a single distrust. With this concentration on the negative aspects of the dreamworld, Troyat's work loses its lightness and explores instead the limits of psychological tension and the unrelenting struggle for domination among his characters. With this shift of emphasis in his fiction, he tends not to profit from the technical complexity apparent in *Faux Jour,* and subordinates the novels to their purely thematic demands. Not until *Le Mort saisit le vif* (1942) does Troyat return to the first-person narrator and play upon the possibilities of a character who is at one and the same time actor and chronicler.

Le Vivier

The critical reaction to Troyat's next novel, *Le Vivier*, of 1935, reflects this loss of momentum. Troyat himself recognizes in *Un si long chemin* that "la critique fut plus partagée que pour *Faux Jour*" ("the critics were more divided than for *Faux Jour*, 69), while Jean Vaudal, again in the *Nouvelle Revue Française*, speaks clearly of an "imperceptible déterioration."[7] He concludes by raising the question of whether the subject matter itself "où l'auteur marque encore sa complaisance pour les lâches aux prises avec les eccentriques, l'a-t-il desservi?"[8] ("did the subject matter, in which the author again shows his sympathy for cowards in the grip of eccentrics, do him a disservice?"). Certainly, Troyat appears to be again going over some of the same ground covered in *Faux Jour*. The novel opens with the illness of the hero, Philippe, an illness which signifies both his physical and moral weakness. To convalesce, he goes to stay with his aunt, Mlle. Pastif, who acts as companion and maid to a rich woman, Madame Chasseglin, in her remote house in the provinces. As Philippe recovers, he comes to appreciate increasingly the comfortable protected life in Madame Chasseglin's house, to the extent that he can no longer bear the thought of returning to the real world. Pretending to share Madame Chasseglin's love of different games of patience, he insinuates himself more and more deeply into the household, until he contrives to supplant his aunt as the old lady's companion. With Mlle. Pastif's departure, he remains as sole beneficiary of the atmosphere of passivity and unreality, until a temporary threat appears in the person of Madame Chasseglin's daughter, Nicole, from Paris. Philippe's attraction to Nicole and his intention to break away and follow her to Paris prove ultimately powerless against Madame Chasseglin's petulant opposition and his own weakness, and the novel ends with Nicole's departure, alone, and Philippe's return to the classification of her mother's games of patience.

In *Le Vivier*, Troyat abandons the ill-defined Parisian setting of *Faux Jour* for an equally indeterminate provincial location. All that is important in the position of Madame Chasseglin's house is that it is removed from Paris, which represents the real world of everyday existence, and is a setting of comforting stagnation. In this way, as the novel progresses, Troyat makes use of the traditional literary stereotype of the provinces as barren and oppressive, established by

Madame Bovary or the plays of Chekhov, but then inverts it into an improbably seductive force. For Mlle. Pastif and, more strongly, her nephew, are victims of that paradox of prison psychology by which the most important function of the bars is to keep the world outside at bay and to guarantee a life of unthinking security within. Such a view can, of course, be held only by a certain psychological type, and here, particularly in the analysis of Philippe, Troyat continues the exploration begun in *Faux Jour* of the moral weakness and passivity of the "raté." In this respect, Philippe represents an extension of Jean, with none of the positive transcendental values of the imagination, and reinforces Troyat's position as a novelist concentrating on abnormality in adolescence. Thus, as the novel advances, the moral weakness symbolized by Philippe's illness and his congenital laziness are developed until he can only accept a limited range of reality, and that in itself highly ritualized, under the protection of Madame Chasseglin. He comes to the point where he can only bear existence in the fish tank of the novel's title and is incapable of living in the fresh waters outside. The episode with Nicole, therefore, represents one final temptation of the outside world, but one he instinctively knows he will refuse, and at no point threatens to divert the narrative to a new direction.

It is highly significant that the only exercise of his will in the novel should be in his rivalry with his aunt for the affections of their employer. Not only is he motivated by the lucid reflection that only with Mlle. Pastif's dismissal will his position be secure, but he operates according to laws observed later by Troyat in his evocations of family life, by which the search for affection becomes the struggle for domination. At the same time, his ambition is more precise: he aims, not merely at eliminating his aunt, but at supplanting her so that he can assume her role in every respect. This coincides with his inevitable decision to abandon Nicole, which, to all intents and purposes, marks the end of his sexuality. In resuming his way of life with Madame Chasseglin after her daughter's departure, he desexualizes himself and becomes, literally and figuratively, an old maid.

The sun about whom Mlle. Pastif and Philippe move is one of Troyat's most grotesque creations, Madame Chasseglin. Modeled upon an American friend of his parents,[9] she becomes transformed, like Kisiakoff in *Tant que la terre durera,* into an exaggeratedly impressive figure, dominating her subjects and devoting herself to her passion for cards. In this context, it is important that the game of cards, while retaining the element of unreal, pointless ritual which characterizes the games in *Faux Jour,* offers an additional ingredient. The American model for Madame Chasseglin and Guillaume both play "belotte," a game which demands two or more players and which at least involves the player in contact with *L'Autre.* The various forms of patience and "réussite," however, are solitary and serve to reinforce the player in his own egoism and to emphasize his self-sufficiency. In the case of Madame Chasseglin, this egoism takes the external form of hypochondria, which links her with the unhealthiness of Philippe, and, more spectacularly, a compulsive urge to dominate those around her—she is the keeper of the "Vivier" and feeds psychologically on those who are her prisoners, first Mlle. Pastif, and then Philippe. In her methods of brutality and blackmail, she looks forward to the adolescent domestic tyrant who is the hero of *L'Araigne.*

What is striking about the novel is the unreality of the atmosphere in which the action occurs, an unreality which is precisely that of the fish tank, in which the glass separates and distorts the interior and exterior worlds. Characteristically, Troyat describes this distorting barrier in terms of theatrical imagery: before Philippe has become enmeshed in the trap, at the beginning of the novel, he writes: "Il se sentait séparé de sa tante et du Madame Chasseglin par l'exhaussement de la lumière qui sépare les acteurs du spectateur enfermé dans l'ombre"[10] ("He felt separated from his aunt and Mme Chasseglin by the raising of the lights which separate the actors from the spectator, still in darkness"). The subject matter of the novel is the very unnaturalness of the setting in which the only inhabitants are, literally, "monstres." The problem, however, is whether the novel goes any further, whether it constitutes anything more than a psychological case study of abnormality. This is the basis of Jean Vaudel's criticism. While recognizing the careful artistry of Troyat the novelist, he objects to the way in which the entire work is unmodulated, remaining on one level of psychological intensity, and he concludes: "On se gardera de chercher, derrière ces pages, de ces valeurs retranchées qui font le poids d'un livre. Celui-ci est léger, mince, mais non par excès de finesse"[11] ("No one will look in these pages for those entrenched values which give a book its weight. This book is light and slim, but not through excessive subtlety"). It is this lack of abstract values, the absence of a wider theoretical context, which separates Troyat from writers such as Green and Mauriac. At the same time, that literary complexity and self-reference which was present in *Faux Jour* has now disappeared: the literary and philosophical possibilities of the card game which generate Louis Guilloux's *Le Jeu de patience* are subordinated to a purely psychological purpose, and the novel is the lighter for it.

Grandeur nature

In his third novel, in 1936, Troyat returns to the exploration of the relationship between father and son outlined in *Faux Jour*, a return which he attributes in *Un si long chemin* to a preoccupation with his own parents and their hardship: "Il est évident qu'à voir mes parents souffrir avec tant de décence dans un pays qui n'était pas le leur, j'ai été sensibilisé aux rapports du père et de l'enfant" ("Obviously, seeing my parents suffering so nobly in a strange country, I was made aware of the relationship between father and son," 72). Thus, in *Grandeur nature* he emphasizes the stultifying effects of a life of poverty, and combines the marginal milieu of *Faux Jour* with the domestic claustrophobia of *Le Vivier*. At the same time, Troyat bases the novel on his own firsthand experiences of the theatrical world as a cinema extra, a procedure which marks an important transition in his development as a novelist. *Grandeur nature* is the first of his novels in which he uses the professional writer's technique of changes in well-researched background detail as the precondition for continuing work. In a body of fiction in which the themes and preoccupations remain constant, the appearance of renewal is conveyed by different settings.

The novel is centered on the character of Antoine Vautier, a middle-aged mediocre actor, who still lives in hope of obtaining the role that will win for him the success he merits. He is working in a period of professional and economic crisis, however, in which the old style of theater is being replaced by modern acting methods and by the cinema, and where work is hard to come by. His sole comfort, as show after show closes, is his family, his wife Jeanne and son Christian, over whom he rules as a spoiled monarch. This comforting, claustrophobic life is changed irremediably when, while seeking a part for himself, he manages to have Christian accepted as the star of a film version of Daudet's novel *Jack*. The success of the film gives Christian immense prestige, both within the theatrical

profession and, more important, within the Vautier family, to the
extent that as an actor and as a father, Antoine is relegated to
a secondary position. His exclusion is felt so painfully that he seeks
refuge in an affair with an actress, Reine Roy, and in a minor role
in a touring company in Provence. He is unable to forget his family,
however, and returns to Paris when Christian's second film is a
disaster, hoping to resume his previous role as head of an adoring
household. But the damage proves to be irreversible and Christian
is still the unshakable center of the family. The novel ends with
Vautier's halfhearted attempt at suicide, interrupted by his wife's
cry for help as she drops the dinner plates. There is no escape from
his domestic limbo.

Vautier is the quintessential portrait of the "raté": now middle-
aged, he has lost his chance of success and can live on only in
mediocrity and self-delusion. He is condemned by the example of
his father, an actor also, who, in spite of constant hard work, never
reached stardom. In the person of Vautier, therefore, Troyat presents
the embodiment of the theatrical imagery he has used previously to
denote unreality and inauthenticity, a feature which adds further
dimension to a character who follows the stereotype of the failed
actor, as, for example, in John Osborne's *The Entertainer*. Through
the profession of acting, Troyat develops his interest in the conflict
between the world of unreality and illusion and the life-sized world
outside the theater with which Vautier finally has to reckon. At the
same time, the inauthenticity of Antoine as actor is reinforced by
his narcissism: the novel opens with him removing makeup in front
of a dressing-room mirror, and mirror images recur throughout the
book. Thus, his inauthenticity and self-delusion as an actor, combined with his self-preoccupation, fit him for the role as unques-
tioned and unquestioning head of his family, which he rules as a
petty tyrant.

The problem, however, lies precisely in Vautier's unconscious-
ness, his automatic acceptance of his family's love and loyalty, and
his failure to recognize that the launching of Christian on a theatrical
career may have unpredictable consequences. In Troyat's fictional
world, the family is not a static entity, but a dynamic organism,
made up of competing, shifting forces. Thus, in financial and professional terms, Christian rapidly displaces Antoine, a change heralded
neatly by a scene at the beginning of the novel in which Christian
plays at rehearsing an episode with Jeanne. This scene also looks

forward to the way in which Jeanne switches her allegiance to her son on his success and, more vigorously still, on his failure, for her subservient nature, so long devoted to Vautier, leads her to abase herself before the most successful member of her family. It is Vautier's tragedy that his mediocrity can compete with Christian neither in the glory of his success nor in the drama of his failure and that his real everyday torment goes unrecognized.

It is also a tragedy which Vautier, unthinkingly, brings upon himself. Once he has convinced Jeanne of the rightness of Christian's entry into the film industry, the action continues irreversibly and escape for Vautier is impossible. His attempt to lose himself in the admiration of Reine Roy is doomed to failure: his obsessive jealousy which renders him ultrasensitive transforms their relationship into a repetition of the one with his wife, a repetition conveyed by the actress's name itself, Reine Roy, a caricature of a theatrical pseudonym. Furthermore, the carefully drawn parallels between the two parts of the novel, where Vautier, in spite of geographical displacement, merely reflects his past actions, imprison him in a situation which is unable to evolve to any resolution of its problems. For Vautier's real world is not the theater but his family, and it is Jeanne and Christian alone who confer meaning upon him. The problem is that, through his initial thoughtless act, that meaning has been lost and he is condemned to live in limbo between a profession in which he is a failure and a family of which he is no longer the center. In this way, obliquely, Troyat approaches one of his major thematic interests, the psychology of exile which he explores here in the restricted context of the family unit.

As a minor domestic tragedy, *Grandeur nature* is a successful novel: carefully constructed, almost entirely generated by its images of mirrors and actors, it moves unremittingly toward the final exile of the hero, an exile he has ironically instituted himself. At the same time, however, Vaudal's criticism of *Le Vivier* could be applied here, to the extent that Troyat appears to be retrenching himself into a perfectly worked but minor fictional genre, in which a limited psychological state is explored and where openings out to broader preoccupations are severely restricted. This feature is connected with a by now established characteristic of Troyat's fiction, the unsympathetic nature of his characters after *Faux Jour*. There is little to engage the reader in the struggle between Madame Chasseglin and Philippe; similarly, Vautier's pompousness, his selfish domination of his family, his unprovoked rages at Reine Roy, all have a childish, petulant quality, not totally relieved by his final depression, from which self-pity is by no means absent. Nor are his family any more attractive: Christian is merely self-centered and precocious; Jeanne oscillates between total self-effacement and overbearing pride in the success of her son. In other words, Troyat has placed his undoubted technical mastery at the service of a story which remains curiously cold. Excellent portrait of domestic exile though it be, *Grandeur nature* has ultimately the attraction of a well-constructed game.

L'Araigne

L'Araigne constitutes Troyat's most successful experiment in the short psychological novel of the interwar and Occupation period. It won for him the Prix Goncourt of 1938, against stiff competition from François de Roux's novel, *Brune,* and automatically increased his readership from his usual four or five thousand to 100,000. At the same time, it went some way toward answering criticism of the previous novels by providing precise psychological and intellectual foundations for his hero's behavior and by escaping from the light confines of the story to raise certain general problems. It was also the novel with which Troyat experienced the most difficulty. He recalls, in *Un si long chemin,* that his initial attempt to follow two parallel subjects, a "personage inadapté, en butte à l'intolérable pression des autres" ("a maladjusted character, exposed to the intolerable pressure of other people") and "une famille composée exclusivement de femmes" ("a family composed exclusively of women," 74), was severely criticized when he showed the manuscript to the "club" of Jean Bassou, Michelle Maurois, Claude Mauriac, and Jean Davray, who insisted that he subordinate the latter theme to the former, moving the hero, Gérard Fonsèque, to the center of the stage.

The novel opens with a description of the Fonsèque family in their gloomy apartment in the place des Vosges: a neurotic mother, three sisters, Elizabeth, Luce, and Marie-Claude, and, at the center of this admiring world, the only son, Gérard. The death of his mother, who has acted as a barrier between Gérard and reality and has denied him nothing, throws him into a state of total disorientation, to which he reacts by retreating further into his world of ideas and by tightening his grip of domination over his sisters. The three successive dramas in the novel concern the successful attempts of Elizabeth, Luce, and Marie-Claude to leave the stultifying *vivier* of the apartment and marry, and the growing desperation of Gérard as he realizes the failure of all his attempts to bring his sisters to heel by poisoning their relationships. His final act of blackmail, to prevent the marriage of Marie-Claude, is to simulate a suicide attempt by taking poison, but he miscalculates the dose and transforms his performance into a real suicide.

The quotation from Marguerite de Navarre which opens the novel, "Gardez-vous de faire comme l'araigne qui convertit toutes les bonnes viandes en venin"[12] ("Do not be like the spider which changes all wholesome meats into poison"), announces the way in which the narrative is to be totally centered on Gérard, in the middle of his web, searching to dominate those around him through his poison. In a very real sense, he is the only character of the novel, a fact reinforced by his own self-preoccupation and narcissism, conveyed in the multiplication of mirror images. In *L'Araigne*, Troyat minimizes the theatrical imagery prevalent in the earlier novels, but accentuates the role of mirrors already exploited in *Grandeur nature*: Gérard does not play a role for other people, because he has no interest in their reactions; his acting is for an audience consisting only of himself. What distinguishes him from earlier characters, particularly Madame Chasseglin and Philippe, with whom he has undoubted affinities, is the way in which Troyat has furnished more concrete intellectual and psychological reasons for his sterility, the "fonds sec" of the family name, and his urge to dominate.

Gérard's life is built upon a belief in the superiority of the intellectual over ordinary humanity. This entitles him to be free of the moral constraints that bind lesser individuals, a concept which he derives from Nietzsche's aphorism in *Also sprach Zarathustra* that "L'homme est quelque chose qui doit être surmonté" ("Man is something which must be overcome," 14). At the same time, his greater intellect permits him to direct the lives of others in what he sees as their best interests. Hence, he plans to control his family, on the basis that "J'ai trop réfléchi, trop travaillé, pour ne pas discerner pour chacun la route à suivre, le danger à éviter, le bonheur à cueillir" ("I have thought and worked too much not to see the way which each of you must follow, the dangers you must avoid, the happiness you must grasp," 15). Quite apart from Troyat's dislike of this philosophy and its plainly inapplicable nature in a domestic context,

he casts considerable doubts on Gérard's credentials as an intellectual. One of his recurrent characteristics is his constant habit of
quotation, a habit which reveals a desire for easy victories in argument and a rigidity of thought and which raises the question of
whether there is any originality behind his use of quotes. Gérard
has incontestably read much, but possibly digested little: certainly
the only real work he undertakes is the translation of English de-
tective novels. Similarly, when faced with concrete problems which
need elucidation, he is surprisingly incapable. When Marie-Claude
is attracted to Gérard's friend, Vigneral, she resorts to the device
of putting on the wall a photograph, not of her lover, but of the
actor Fred Colmar, "qui ressemblait à Vigneral" ("who looked like
Vigneral," 188): Gérard, the intellectual, never succeeds in decoding
the significance of the picture. Finally, if his real cleverness is under
suspicion, his ability to cope with the implications of his elitist
philosophy is also seriously impaired. Like Dostoevski's Raskolni-
kov, in *Crime and Punishment*, Gérard has adopted the role of the
superman when what he really craves is exactly the opposite, comfort
and protection.

This raises the question that Gérard's intellectuality and will to
superiority are derived from purely psychological factors, and in this
context it is important that Troyat has once again concentrated on
the specific problems of the adolescent, in which immature, over-
dogmatic intellectual positions are mingled with psychological insecurity. He insists upon the causal effects of Gérard's neurotic,
overprotective mother, who communicates her neurosis to her son
in the form of a constant need for exclusive attention and affection.
This neurosis is compounded by the presence of the sisters whom
he idealizes as part of his own life, to the extent that, as Troyat
notes in *Un si long chemin*, "il serait inconsciemment amoureux de
ses soeurs. Il ne supporterait pas de les savoir exposées aux vulgaires
tentations des sens" ("he is unconsciously in love with his sisters
and cannot bear knowing them exposed to vulgar sensual tempta-
tions," 74). This Oedipal relationship, first to his mother, then
transferred to Elizabeth, Luce, and, particularly Marie-Claude, inevitably takes the form of intense sexual possessiveness and jealousy,
and has the effect of nullifying his own sexual urges. The novel
contains two scenes of explicit sexual fiasco, one with school friends
in a brothel, the other in his apartment with a girl, Tina, and it
becomes clear that the urge to dominate others, supported by his

philosophical elitism, is merely, in Adlerian terms, an exaggerated compensation for weakness and inferiority. With no authentic intellectual position, therefore, and an extreme psychological sickness grounded in vulnerability, it is inevitable that Gérard, enclosed in his own world of mirrors, will ultimately poison only himself, while his web remains too fragile to trap for long the healthy individuals who surround him.

In this way, more than *Le Vivier* or *Grandeur nature*, which remain imprisoned in their world of failure, *L'Araigne* opens out toward the establishment of general positive values. The gloomy claustrophobia of the apartment in the place des Vosges is there to be escaped and exchanged for a healthy life in the real world. Elizabeth, Luce, and Marie-Claude obviously owe much to Chekhov's *Three Sisters*, but succeed in asserting their normality and their autonomy. It is upon the sick member of the family, Gérard, that the apartment exerts its fascination, a fascination reflected in the intellectual stance he adopts. In *L'Araigne*, Troyat indicates for the first time that general distrust of intellectuality which characterizes much of his later work and is at its most acerbic in *La Tête sur les épaules*, where another intellectual adolescent is at work destroying the lives of those around him. Troyat's distrust is based, first, on a refusal of the fashionable and oversimplified Nietzscheanism of the 1930s, and in this respect, Gérard follows the path of Gide's *Immoraliste*, Michel, who cannot cope with the philosophy he has chosen and ends up by destroying his wife and himself. More broadly, however, the novel constitutes an indictment of any life ruled purely by ideas, in which the emotional world is lacking. At this point, Troyat opposes his humble value of acceptance and happiness which motivates much of his later work. On the death of Gérard, at the sight of this "intellectuel raté, aigri, malade" ("failed, bitter and sick intellectual," 240), his friend Lequesne, who has married Luce, concludes, "la vie ne s'obtient pas, elle s'accepte" ("life is not conquered, it is accepted," 241), a philosophy which contradicts so much of French 1930s metaphysical writing and which reveals a profound fatalism central to Troyat's literary production.

This entry into a general discussion of ideas and contrast of opposing values marks a new departure in Troyat's short fiction and takes it as near as it will come to French philosophical novels of the interwar years. That this step was still too hesitant is confirmed by Marcel Arland's review of *L'Araigne*, in which he praises the subject matter, but regrets that "son histoire est-elle trop rapide et n'atteint-elle pas à l'ampleur qu'on eût souhaitée"[13] ("His story is too fast and does not attain the weight one would have liked"). He continues, "Le livre se développe en péripéties plutôt qu'en profondeur"[14] ("The book develops episodically rather than in depth"), and concludes by an extraordinarily exact description of the novel, which applies also to all the short fiction: "ce qui limite un peu son livre . . . c'est peut-être qu'il se contente trop facilement d'être une histoire, un beau suject fort bien exposé"[15] ("what slightly limits his book is the fact that it is perhaps too easily satisfied with being a story, a fine subject well told"). In other words, Troyat's insistence on his role as storyteller militates in favor of superficiality and against depth: his fiction is still subjected to the tyranny of the subject.

Judith Madrier

Judith Madrier occupies an anomalous position in Troyat's fictional work. Written from October to December 1939, and describing the events of the "Phony War," it constitutes his only attempt to transpose contemporary history into fictional form. His treatment of the same period in La Rencontre is done with a gap of eighteen years between the events and their reconstruction and falls more into the category of the historical novel. It is perhaps for this reason that Troyat has subsequently repudiated the novel, dismissing it as a "travail de circonstance,"[16] and has never allowed it to be reprinted. Since this is the only novel to be thus excluded from the canon of his fiction, it acquires some considerable importance as a literary curiosity and as an indicator of Troyat's literary taste and ambitions.

The novel opens with Charles and Judith Madrier traveling in a troop train to Charles's appointment in the "Intendance" of a garrison in the Massif Central. As the journey continues through the night, Troyat uses a series of flashbacks to record Charles's role as a worthy but boring grain merchant, his infatuation and marriage with Judith, manipulated by her sinister and cunning mother, Madame Fleck, and her subsequent infidelity with a young man, Lescure, now mobilized on the Franco-German border. The declaration of war brings Judith temporarily back to a sense of her responsibilities, and in a moment of patriotic fervor she ends the affair with Lescure and decides to accompany Charles to his posting. Once in the small provincial town, however, her dissatisfaction returns, fueled by

Charles's complacency and clumsiness and by her fears for Lescure's life. In her state of boredom, she succumbs to the advances of a strong, cynical businessman, the sinisterly named Mauser, and begins to lead a double life. This domestic "drôle de guerre" is ended by an anonymous letter, informing Charles of his wife's infidelity, and by Judith's own confession. Her despair is rendered complete by the news of the death of Lescure on patrol in the Vosges, and she leaves with Mauser for the south of France. It is this which finally shakes Charles out of his lethargy. Having previously avoided being sent to the Front, thus earning Judith's contempt, he now asks for an immediate posting and, as he goes off to the real war, experiences for the first time a sense of freedom and value.

The novel raises the same problem as that posed by the first draft of *L'Araigne*, the ambition to follow two ultimately separate destinies adequately in fictional form. Whereas the obvious model for the novel, *Madame Bovary*, is able to combine the careers of Charles and Emma by making them both victims of the same economic and social forces, *Judith Madrier* ends with the protagonists going their separate ways in such a manner as to show their marriage as a momentary coalition. In Judith herself, Troyat has combined elements of Emma Bovary and Mauriac's Thérèse Desqueyroux. Like Emma, she marries out of boredom and drifts into affairs in the illusory hope of finding meaning in change. Similarly, her attempts at self-realization are frustrated by an innate laziness: she is unable even to lose herself in literature because she grows bored with the length of the books she reads. In one important respect, however, she differs from her Flaubertian predecessor: she lacks the romantic world view which renders Emma's tragedy so poignant and so grandiose. Mauser, who first seduces Judith during an automobile excursion to a forest, never possesses even the false charisma of Rodolphe: the disabused heroine sees him immediately for what he is, a self-seeking, shady businessman, well on his way to collaboration, and her affair with him takes the form of a conscious revenge against Charles. In this way, she ressembles Thérèse Desqueyroux more than Emma, imprisoned with a good but unbearable husband, chain smoking, and even contemplating murdering him by poison. The ending of the novel, in which she departs with Mauser, is a reflection of Emma's suicide, but a more precise reference to Thérèse's departure for Paris which promises merely a continuation of the moral desert in which she has been living. In his portrayal of Judith,

therefore, Troyat relies upon the previous patterns established by
Flaubert and Mauriac to present a convincing analysis of a woman
who discovers her true love too late and who feels herself so imprisoned in her marriage with a man she comes to despise that she
becomes morally dead and accepts the most damning form of escape
when it is offered, because it constitutes at least a break with
mediocrity.

The importance of Charles lies less in his unbending mediocre
goodness, than in his final liberation from himself, in terms which
bring the novel close to the language of contemporary French philosophical fiction. Troyat is at pains to stress Charles's debt to his
namesake in *Madame Bovary*: "En présence de ces deux femmes, le
malheureux était gêné par sa grande taille, par son visage ferme et
rouge de paysan, par sa voix forte, par ses pieds nux aux orteils
massifs"[17] ("In the presence of these two women, the wretch was
embarrassed by his height, his strong red peasant's face, his loud
voice, his bare feet with enormous toenails"); similarly, Charles as
an officer is as unconvincing as Charles Bovary as a doctor, a fact
signified by his tight-fitting uniform. Yet, whereas his wife reflects
Emma's failure, Charles, at the last moment, is able to save himself
by assuming his full responsibility. His decision to replace his colleague Plot at the Front is not to be read as a mirror image of
Judith's retreat to the Côte d'Azur. It is not a suicide, but an
affirmation of life. As Troyat writes at the end of the novel, "Il
veut vivre. Vivre de toutes ses forces, vivre comme il n'a pas encore
vécu, vivre comme un *autre*, vivre comme *les autres*" ("He wants to
live, to live with all his strength, to live like he has never lived,
to live like another person, to live like other people," 247), and
his journey to the Front becomes an escape from his old self, defined
by Judith, and a liberation of metaphysical dimensions. The final
description of Charles records his ambition to "retomber dans la
masse des hommes" ("to fall back into the mass of humanity," 248),
and, in a phrase which looks forward to the ending of Sartre's *La
Mort dans l'âme*, notes, "Il est libre, il est neuf, il est sauvé" ("He
is free, he is new, he is saved," 247). Charles's rejection of his
mediocrity in favor of action in the front line, therefore, has explicit
existential significance: by choosing, he has freed himself and become authentic.

In case the full meaning of Charles's mediocrity and subsequent
salvation is not immediately apparent, Troyat chooses to underline

it by introducing a young officer, Villers, a student, who situates the problem in a theological context of the equal Manichean struggle between God and the Devil. In statements which look forward to *Le Signe du taureau* and particularly the stories in *Le Geste d'Eve* (Eve's gesture), Villers expounds his view of the Devil as the embodiment, not of spectacular evil, but of stultifying mediocrity, "Le diable, c'est le juste milieu atroce de l'humanité" ("The Devil is the terrible average of humanity," 104), and warns, "Gardez-vous de manquer de coeur" ("Beware of losing all emotion," 198). His own rejection of the comfortable life behind the lines and his decision to volunteer for active service increases Judith's contempt for Charles and prefigures his own solution at the end of the novel.

Troyat's dissatisfaction with the novel is, in some respects, comprehensible. While the body of the work presents an interesting evocation of French military life in the provinces in the months before the German invasion, its ending, with Charles rushing to support the troops in the east, has an element of propaganda and jingoism about it. Nor is the novel by any means a complete technical success. It reads all too often as a compilation of three separate strands: Judith's descent into despair, Charles's salvation in action, and the metaphysical commentary embodied in Villers. In this way, it attempts to be a realist psychological novel and a philosophical novel at the same time, without being able to fuse together the isolated elements. Finally, while the work gains weight from its transparent allusions to Flaubert and Mauriac, these references are too intrusive and render the skeleton of the narrative too apparent. Nevertheless, Troyat's criticism is unduly harsh and is probably based upon the way in which the novel was rushed into print before the rewriting which perfected *L'Araigne* could be undertaken. It was precisely this rewriting which permitted a fusion of two elements, Gérard and the sisters, and such an operation on *Judith Madrier* would undoubtedly have merged the destinies of Charles and Judith more satisfyingly, as well as muting the overt literary allusions and the metaphysical rhetoric. Yet, if Troyat's regret concerns the fact that he was led by events to depart from his familiar field of tightly enclosed psychological tension for a more didactic fiction, he is mistaken. In comparison with *Le Vivier*, *Grandeur nature*, and *L'Araigne*, *Judith Madrier*, with all its imperfections, presents a solid world in which liberation is possible, and where the fiction may open out into abstraction. The freedom of Charles at the end of the novel is that of the reader as well, a freedom not to be felt again in Troyat's short fiction, which is possibly diminished for that very reason.

Le Mort saisit le vif

Like *Le Vivier*, *Le Mort saisit le vif* has its basis in Troyat's own experience. His friend, Volodia Bylinine, was killed in the Battle of France and his wife showed Troyat his private notebooks.[18] What impressed Troyat was not simply the emotion at reading his dead friend's work, but also the narrative possibilities of a plagiarist who would pass off such work as his own. In *Le Mort saisit le vif* Troyat explores this complex subject by returning for the last time in his short fiction to the first-person narrator, a procedure which accentuates the complexity and helps to produce one of his richest works.

The novel's main character is Jacques Sorbier, who is to the world of letters what Antoine Vautier is to the theater, a mediocre practitioner of the art, working as the editor of a children's comic, the *Rataplan*, in which, like the hero of Jean Renoir's film *Le Crime de Monsieur Lange*, he publishes lurid tales of Arizona. This comfortable, if ultimately unsatisfying existence is overturned by his marriage to Suzanne, the widow of his boyhood friend Georges Galard. It is Suzanne who takes over his life by persuading him to publish under his own name the manuscript of a novel by her first husband, a novel which, written by a doctor and a work of extreme populism, has obvious affinities with Céline's *Voyage au bout de la nuit*. Sorbier protests, but finally gives in to the suggestion, hoping that the novel will sink without trace. Instead, it becomes a literary event, winning the prestigious Prix Maupassant and turning Sorbier into a celebrity. Half-pleased and half-frightened at his success, he gradually adopts the persona of Galard while at the same time experiencing a sense of remorse and a need to confess. This need is finally met when the model for the main character of the novel, Nicole Domini, confronts him, but even confession to her cannot alter the falsity of his public position. His attempt to assert his own identity by publishing his own work as a second novel fails when it is rejected by the publishers: the only possibility that remains is to continue the deception by bringing out an edition based on Galard's letters to Suzanne. It is at this point, however, that escape from inauthenticity becomes possible, as Sorbier realizes that Suzanne is still in love with Galard and is merely fashioning him into an image of her former husband so that she can continue that love. The novel ends with Sorbier concluding his letter to Suzanne and leaving his marriage and his false life.

Clearly, in many respects *Le Mort saisit le vif* explores areas already covered in the previous novels. Again, the central character is a "raté," like Guillaume in *Faux Jour* and Antoine Vautier in *Grandeur nature*. His wife, Suzanne, appears initially to share the same blind worship of success as Jeanne Vautier. The life that the two lead is inauthentic, both in the marriage itself and in the operation of sustaining the deception, a feature which entails the continued use of theater and actor images together with an insistence on the role of the mirror, not for narcissim or self-delusion, but as a constant reminder and reproach of inescapable reality. At the same time, to disguise this repetition of established features, Troyat uses the same technique as that employed in *Grandeur nature* of providing a particular concrete setting for his action: the world of Parisian publishing and the events surrounding the award of a major literary prize, in which he transposes his own experience of the Prix Goncourt.

The novel, however, is much more than the narration of a familiar situation in a new setting and marks a very real departure toward complexity and density in Troyat's fiction. The relationship between the dead Galard and Jacques Sorbier, who strives to both resemble his model and retain his distance from him, introduces the disturbing theme of the double which he has already explored in "Monsieur Citrine," and which owes much to the fantastic elements of E. T. A. Hoffmann, Gogol, and Dostoevski. In *Le Mort saisit le vif* this theme appears in two ways: the, literally, split personality of Sorbier, conveyed perfectly by a scene in which he looks at his own reflection in a taxi mirror and comments, "la glace intérieure du taxi est fêlée et ça me fait deux visages mal soudés à la machoire"[19] ("the inside mirror of the taxi is cracked and gives me two faces, imperfectly welded together at the jaw"), and the way in which Galard constitutes a *Doppelgänger*, the very presence of death overshadowing Sorbier, his own dead self who, if he cannot be shaken off, will have to be seen and will destroy him. Closely connected to the literary theme of the double is Troyat's use of the ghost story, by which Galard does not merely superficially haunt Sorbier but, like an incubus, has found his second home in Sorbier's body and is living through him.

At the same time, both Sorbier and Suzanne have a depth of
character absent in the earlier novels. Suzanne is revealed to be much
more than the extension of Jeanne Vautier that she initially appears:
she exploits the weakness, the very greyness of Sorbier for a high
purpose, the re-creation of her dead husband by means of a Pyg-
malion-like transformation. Similarly, while earlier portraits of the
"raté" are static and permit no evolution, Jacques Sorbier develops
toward the point of his final triumph. He begins by being easily
persuaded by Suzanne and by experiencing a complex mixture of
guilt and pleasure at the success of what he half believes to be his
own book. Subsequently, he is beset by two anxieties: that he will
be unable to repeat the performance on his own talent alone, thus
calling into question his entire role, and that his "crime" needs
confession and absolution. In this aspect of the novel, Troyat enters
a complex psychological and moral area, already debated in "Le
Jugement de Dieu" of 1941. Although Sorbier is able to confess
his guilt to Nicole Domini, he has paid his debt only on purely
literary terms, to "un personnage de roman qui a voulu connaître
son auteur" ("a character of a novel who wanted to know her author,"
109). Real absolution can only be obtained through punishment,
and punishment can only be metered out by Sorbier's father, a fact
which reinforces the hero's retarded weakness. The problem, however, is that the father is a pathetic figure who needs protection,
not confrontation, and Jacques cannot bring himself to confess to
him. He is caught, therefore, in the same trap as the hero of "Le
Jugement de Dieu" by which, without judgment, there can be no
escape from guilt.

It is this trap which forces Sorbier to discover his own willpower
and provide his own judgment on himself, and it is this which
constitutes the real originality of the novel. His final break with
Suzanne and the constraining presence of Galard is announced by
an initial movement of self-assertion, when his employer at the
Rataplan, horrified by the "sombres révélations de ce roman populiste" ("the somber revelations of this populist novel," 58), demands that he take a pseudonym. Sorbier, unwilling to hide behind
yet another mask, refuses and is dismissed. This early attempt to
fight his way back to reality reaches its successful conclusion with
Jacques's realization of the constant nature of Suzanne's love for
Galard and his own role as substitute in the whole affair of the
books. His decision to leave Suzanne and his life of lies is the closest

that Troyat comes to an existentialist position in his fiction, by which "mauvaise foi," which Sartre too describes in theatrical terms,[20] is rejected in favor of authenticity. At the same time, Sorbier's departure constitutes an escape from an atmosphere dominated by death, an atmosphere fostered and exploited by Suzanne, and an affirmation of the values of life.

This psychological and thematic depth is reinforced by the unusual textual complexity of the novel, which derives from the fact that it takes the form of a long letter addressed to Suzanne explaining Sorbier's decision to leave. Psychologically, it represents the only form of communication open to Sorbier: in their conversation, he is either totally dominated or resorts to incoherent exclamation. In writing, he achieves the only form of confession of which he is capable. Similarly, it is only by writing that he is able to effect a break with his false situation: the careful enumeration of events and emotions, which constitute an authentic mirror of Sorbier's life, moves logically toward an ending which, although literary in nature, must entail a resolution of the problems in his real life. Finally, the heroic affirmation of authenticity and life embodied in Sorbier's departure is mirrored by the fact that the journal-letter to Suzanne has become the authentic novel he was unable to write and the revenge of his previous literary mediocrity. By refusing Galard's letters to Suzanne and, instead, writing his own, he has laid the ghost: the very existence of the novel is Sorbier's finest act of self-affirmation.

The range and atmosphere of *Le Mort saisit le vif* take it very close to Troyat's novellas and short stories, in which a relaxation of the constraints of the claustrophobic psychological novels permits a lighter touch and a deeper textual awareness. Ultimately, in the postwar short fiction, the limitations of the genre prove too strong, and he moves back into the concrete world of psychological realism. Before that retreat, however, he provides his most ample discussion of the conflict between dream and reality in the struggles of the businessman Germain Laugier, the hero of *Le Signe du taureau*, a conflict in which the dream life is definitively defeated.

Le Signe du taureau

This preoccupation with a conflict in the evaluation of the importance of the dream is conveyed immediately by the statement at the beginning of the novel: "Le second signe du zodiaque est le signe du taureau. C'est celui des personnes ennemies du rêve et attachées aux plaisirs substantiels"[21] ("The second sign of the zodiac is that of Taurus the bull, the sign of people hostile to the dream-world and attached to concrete enjoyment"). This enemy of the dream life is the novel's hero, Germain Laugier, a successful shoe manufacturer whose secure, solid existence with his wife Alice is temporarily overturned by the return to his life of an ex-mistress, Edith. This, in its turn, prompts Laugier to neglect his business and to re-create his life as a poor artist before he took the road to commercial success. He begins to frequent his old haunts on the Left Bank again and renews contact with an old sculptor-friend, Bourdieu, who in turn introduces him to his protégé, Maurice Gèvres. The novel then follows two separate but interlinking lines of development: Laugier's meeting with Edith and their realization that a love-affair between them is now impossible; the life of the lonely and hypersensitive Gèvres, who sees his beloved sculpture rejected by the Salon and seeks comfort with Laugier's wife. The denouement is prompted by Laugier's return home after the break with Edith to discover Gèvres and Alice deep in conversation. He vents his frustrations upon the sculptor, gratuitously insulting him and throwing him out of his house. In despair, Gèvres returns to his studio and hangs himself, while Laugier, now liberated from his bohemian past, enthusiastically resumes command of his empire.

The novel which, on the surface, recounts the banal story of the return of a character from the hero's past, a device which Troyat uses again in *Une Extrême amitié*, has its significance in the implications of commitment to the dreamworld. Initially, Germain Laugier who in many respects ressembles Duhamel's tycoon Joseph Pasquier, is completely rooted in the real world, unthinkingly governing the affairs of his shoe factory. This unthinking exercise of power is conveyed by the sheer size and brute strength of the character who, quite literally, ressembles the zodiacal bull: Troyat emphasises his "corps massif" ("his massive body," 49) and his "visage massif, au menton doublé, aux rides saines" ("his massive face, with a double chin and healthy wrinkles," 72). The physical portrait of Laugier comes to resemble that given by Simenon of the hero of *L'Ecluse No. 1*, another all-powerful businessman whose secret lies in his past life. It is from this position of power and unthinking strength that Laugier's excursion into the dreamworld begins, a dreamworld which Troyat is at pains to depict in its precise composite parts. In one respect, that life is merely Laugier's past, endowed with all the attractiveness that nostalgia can bestow upon it. More specifically, it is connected with Laugier's participation in the free and uninhibited world of "la bohême," whose somewhat stereotypical depiction has progressed little from Murger. Finally, Laugier's entry into the life of dreams is indissolubly linked with his attempt to resurrect his never-consummated affair with Edith, an attempt doomed to failure because the affair lies in the past and cannot be brought into the present. As Edith mournfully points out to Germain: "Entre toi et moi, il y a un fantôme de toi, un fantôme de moi" ("Between you and me, there is your ghost and my ghost," 301).

The reference to ghosts, however, serves to remind the reader that, while the dream life is for Laugier a mere interlude, for other characters, like Gèvres, it can be a powerfully sinister force. For the sculptor is one of Troyat's adolescents, sensitive, vulnerable, and isolated in an acute bohemian poverty, and the reasons for his death concern both his own psychology and darker forces to which his personality is subjected. On a realist plane, his suicide can be attributed to his despair at the rejection of his sculpture and, more precisely, his humiliation in front of Alice at the hands of Laugier, an event which convinces him of the degeneracy of the whole human race. At the same time, Troyat expands this realist context in order to introduce preoccupations of a supernatural order. The model for Gèvres's sculpture is a young circus boy whose mother, the sinister Madame Morelli, demands that he make love with her in exchange for her son's services. Gèvres's refusal so angers her that she sets to casting a spell upon him, invoking the power of the Devil to give her revenge. In this way, one of the main characters of the short stories enters the novel, providing a dark background to the action in which forces for good and evil struggle over man's destiny, and it is Gèvres's final vision of a world in which the Devil has won that leads him to hang himself.

In its reflection of the dream life, therefore, the novel appears to reject the position of both characters: Maurice Gèvres is already so isolated from the world that he exists only on an absolute plane and is highly vulnerable to the extreme forces of the imagination. He is the embodiment of the warning given by the Contrôleur in Giraudoux's *Intermezzo*, "Ne touchez pas aux bornes de la vie humaine"[22]

("Do not touch the limits of human life"), for, beyond the limits of ordinary existence lies the power of death. At the same time, Laugier's position as "ennemi du rêve" is hardly condoned. Unlike the hero of René Clair's film A nous la liberté, he is unable to transform the return of the past into a permanent change of his life. Similarly, while Troyat's statement, "Il avait perdu des années à poursuivre un rêve insaisissable" ("He had wasted years in pursuing an impossible dream," 74), seems a precise echo of the ending of F. Scott Fitzgerald's The Great Gatsby, Laugier lacks the tragic commitment of Gatsby to that dream. Rather, his return to the bohemian past resembles nothing so much as the brief excursion into the dreamworld of Sinclair Lewis's Babbitt, who leaves the twin cities of Zenith and Monarch for a magic girl, but survives to run his real-estate business with renewed fervor. Laugier's return to the fold and Troyat's reaction to it are conveyed in the last lines of the novel, "Sur les conseils de M. Dupouy de Signac, Germain Laugier a commencé une collection de timbres-poste" ("On the advice of M. Dupouy de Signac, Germain Laugier has started a stamp collection," 316), in which the deliberate switch to the perfect tense is a specific echo of the change of tense at the end of Madame Bovary which announces Homais's victory.

Concerned at the dangers of an absolutist position of a Gèvres, but despising the reintegration into bourgeois order of a Laugier, Troyat proposes a middle way of sane humanist recognition of fantasy in the person of the sculptor Bourdieu who, after all, acts as the intermediary between the two men. It is to Bourdieu, the artisanal artist, "une sorte de bûcheron qui croirait aux fées" ("a sort of woodcutter who believed in fairies," 21), and the representative of the author in the novel, that the book's modest humanist message is given: "Par instants, même, il trouvait que la vie était douce et que les hommes valaient mieux que leur réputation" ("At times, even, he found that life was sweet and that men were worth more than their reputation," 314).

In spite of the way in which Troyat continues the preoccupations of Le Mort saisit le vif with positive general values, Le Signe du taureau does not possess the previous novel's technical perfection. For a postwar novel, there is a certain dated quality about the work, still evoking the prewar world, which is reminiscent of the continuation of Romains's Les Hommes de bonne volonté and Duhamel's La Chronique des Pasquier after the hiatus of the Occupation.[23] At the same time, it is not clear that the two narrative elements of the novel, the destinies of Laugier and Gèvres, totally match. To a certain extent, Troyat has committed the same fault as in *Judith Madrier* and the first draft of *L'Araigne*, and followed too many differing elements, with overcontrastive atmospheres. Finally, although he states in *Un si long chemin* that "je me sentais enclin à diversifier mon propos, à éclaircir ma palette" ("I wanted to diversify my subject-matter and lighten my palette," 97), it is by no means certain that *Le Signe du taureau* constitutes any appreciable technical advance.

In one respect at least, however, the novel contains an admirable piece of writing, which shows a high degree of artistry on Troyat's part. The Laugiers' maid, Marie, has just broken off her affair with a circus man, Zucco. A morbid mythomaniac, Marie enjoys imagining her romantic death at the hands of her lover and, indeed, her mutilated body is later found in the metro. Through this very minor subplot, Troyat contrives to link many major aspects of his narrative: Marie, like Edith, becomes "livrée . . . à sa légende" ("given up to her legend," 267); the clandestine nature of the affair between Laugier and Edith is consecrated by the release they feel traveling together in the metro, a device repeated in the title story of *Le Geste d'Eve*; Zucco's profession as circus man connects him with Gèvres and Madame Morelli; and the unhealthy dream life of Marie reflects the negative, death-orientated aspect of the imagination which the novel fully rejects.

Le Signe du taureau sums up Troyat's achievement in the field of short fiction during the interwar years and the Occupation. He has been able to progress beyond a study of the conflict between authenticity and "mauvaise foi" ("bad faith") and the struggle for domination in an unhealthy claustrophobic setting toward a positive solution in the acceptance of "bonheur" and a fruitful awareness of the textual complexity of the short novel form. At the same time, the inability to deal with an extended cast of characters and the increasingly traditional nature of the narrative raise doubts as to whether the genre itself will permit Troyat to renew himself without encroaching on the material of the short stories or the *romans-fleuves*. As Marcel Arland wrote in 1938, "Il a des dons, de l'habileté, du bonheur; ce serait bien le diable s'il manquait la partie"[24] ("He is gifted, clever, and lucky: it would indeed be unfortunate if he failed the test"): the answer is provided by his second period of short fiction, from 1952 onward.

Chapter Three
Novels 1951–80

La Tête sur les épaules

Between the publication of *Le Signe du taureau* in 1945 and the appearance of Troyat's next short novel, *La Tête sur les épaules*, there is a gap of six years, in which he completed the novel cycle *Tant que la terre durera*, experimented in the theater and journalism, and traveled to America. After this diversification of interests, however, *La Tête sur les épaules* does not constitute the expected thematic and technical advance on the previous short fiction. Rather, it marks a regression, formally and psychologically, to the "monstres" of the 1930s and fails to build on the technical complexity deployed in *Le Mort saisit le vif* and *Le Signe du taureau*. Nevertheless, the novel is original in one respect, in that, for the first time, it brings into Troyat's short fiction a concern with immediate issues of contemporary intellectual history. As Troyat recounts to Maurice Chavardès,[1] he had originally wanted to write a novel based upon the son of the revolutionary Joseph Le Bon, who terrorized the Department of the Pas-de-Calais in 1794 and finally died himself on the guillotine. After the morally tormenting period of the Occupation and the Liberation, Troyat decided to transpose the story into a contemporary setting, with an adolescent hero disorientated by the political changes he had just witnessed and imbued with the new philosophical fashion of Sartrean existentialism.

This hero is Etienne Martin, a young intellectual who lives with his mother, Marion, in their small apartment almost taken over by her dress-making business. Etienne's existence is completely changed when he discovers, and subsequently proves, that his father, who was divorced from his mother in 1940, had not died in a road-accident at the end of the war, as he had always been told, but had been executed for guiding political refugees over the Pyrenees to Spain and murdering them on the way. The complex role of being the son of a murderer now dominates Etienne's life and feeds his intellectual inclinations toward the existentialist rejection of convention and morality. At the same time, it poisons his relationship with his mother, just at the moment when Marion is planning to remarry. Terrified at the change in his life that this will bring, Etienne visits Marion's fiancé, her employer Maxime Joubert, and threatens to kill him if he will not write a letter breaking off the engagement. This Joubert does, but only in the knowledge that, confronted by his mother's unhappiness, Etienne will be unable to fulfill his threat and will accept his new situation.

Quite clearly, the novel depends totally upon the characterization of Etienne Martin, a characterization formed of three components which do not, however, entirely interconnect. Troyat's excursion into the novel of ideas takes with it the familiar material of the psychological novel which it is not always able to logically apply. The relationship between Etienne and his mother is a case in point: by seeking to reserve for himself sole access to Marion, Etienne is merely repeating the unhealthy adolescent urge to dominate already expressed in *L'Araigne*. Similarly, this emotional urge for domination and protection is masked by philosophical and intellectual pretensions. What is not clear, however, is why a general exposition and discussion of those pretensions, the postwar vogue of existentialism, should be based on such a particular emotional life. In other words, the validity of the intellectual critique is impaired by the abnormal psychological component of the novel.

A similar confusion is apparent in Troyat's use of the dead father. In the first place, it is unclear why the father's motivation for the crimes should be so mysterious. In the account of the trial which Etienne unearths in the Bibliothèque nationale, it is emphasized that money is not the principal motive and that the murders have an almost gratuitous quality. This dismissal of the money motive undoubtedly adds status to Etienne, while the lack of motivation could be seen to place Louis Martin in a literary-philosophical tradition running from Gide's Lafcadio to Camus's Meursault. Yet so little emphasis is placed upon this that the mystery of the father remains an outstanding, unresolved element of the novel. What is important on the psychological level, however, is that the father is twice dead: removed from the family once by divorce and again, definitively, by execution. With the absent father, Troyat explores his favorite psychological state, that of the weak domineering individual brought up in a world of women and refusing to leave or permit the change of that comforting world. It is ironic in the context of this particular novel that Troyat should consistently view the fact of being brought up by the mother alone as leading to a stultifying mother dependency, whereas Sartre, in *Les Mots,* recalls that the absence of the father was the precondition for a life of freedom, removed from the constraints of the superego. It is the imprisonment which interests Troyat, however, the fixation on the mother threatened by Maxime Joubert.

The discovery of his father's guilt evokes a dual, almost contradictory response in Etienne. On the one hand, the realization that he is the son of a mysterious murderer separates him in his own eyes from the mass of humanity, conferring on him a particularity which becomes indistinguishable from superiority. The crimes of his father serve to place Etienne beyond the pale of bourgeois morality and social convention, and thus may be seen to possess an illusory liberating quality. At the same time, Etienne's discovery frightens him, both in the way in which it operates a social *déclassement,* as Guillaume's mythomania socially alienates Jean in *Faux Jour,* and, more important, by its imprisoning quality as a psychologically determining force. In other words, the son of a murderer is free, in that he is excluded or excludes himself from society, but he is also chained to the fear that the son of a murderer must murder in his own turn. It is for this reason that Etienne's opposition to his mother's remarriage takes the form of a halfhearted murder attempt on her fiancé: Etienne believes, or forces himself to believe, that the murderous mantle of his father is upon him in the same way that the dead Georges Galard controls the writer Jacques Sorbier in *Le Mort saisit le vif.*

This mixture of psychological dependency and self-aggrandizement is continued in Etienne's philosophical inclinations. In this, he resembles closely Gérard Fonsèque of *L'Araigne,* who confuses his selfish domination of his sisters with the espousal of an elitist philosphical creed. Yet, in Fonsèque, Troyat merely sketches a generalized outline of vaguely Nietzschean intellectuality, whereas in *La Tête sur les épaules,* particularly through the character of Etienne's influential philosophy teacher, Thuillier, his target is much more specific: the attraction of French existentialism in the immediate postwar years. In this context, it is important to distinguish immediately between the psychological and propagandist purposes of

Troyat's picture of existentialism. As it is portrayed in the novel, the existentialist fashion, with its belief in elitism and unconventionality, reinforces admirably the character of Etienne, in that it justifies precisely his disorientation at the truth about his father and his horror at his mother's remarriage. As a serious discussion, however, the philosophical portrait is by no means satisfying.

Troyat himself is at pains to deny a direct criticism of existentialism, yet his denial merely reinforces the precise nature of the attack. Asked whether his novel constituted an attack on the existentialists, he replies, in *Un si long chemin:* "En aucune façon! Si mon Etienne Martin avait vécu à une autre époque, je l'aurais placé dans le sillage d'Auguste Comte, de Nietzsche, de Bergson, de Teilhard de Chardin, que sais-je?" ("Not at all! If Etienne Martin had been born in another era, I should have put him under the influence of, let's say, Auguste Comte, Nietzsche, Teilhard de Chardin," 142). Yet he adds: "en 1950, un jeune homme comme lui, avec son inquiétude, sa soif de comprendre, sa peur d'avancer, devait être attiré par la philosphie existentialiste" ("in 1950, a young man like him, with his anxiety, his thirst for understanding, his fear of going forward, would have been attracted by the existentialist philosophy," 142). The existentialist enemy in the novel is therefore the most topical manifestation of that exaggerated intellectuality which Troyat has always condemned: the novel is not "un pamphlet dirigé contre les maîtres de l'existentialisme, mais la dénonciation des dangers de la philosophie quelle qu'elle soit lorsqu'elle se transforme en une règle aveugle, tyrannique et prétend expliquer les manifestations les plus inexplicables de la vie" ("a pamphlet against the leaders of existentialism, but the denunciation of the dangers of any philosophy which becomes transformed into a blind tyrannical system, believing that it can explain the most inexplicable elements in life, 143).

This antagonism to a system-building philosophy tends to place Troyat in a conservative literary tradition, particularly in his portrayal of the *professeur de philosophie* Thuillier, who fulfills the dangerous function, like the philosopher in Bourget's *Le Disciple* or the philosophy teacher in Barrès *Les Déracinés's,* of inculcating into the young and inexperienced ideas which they are not strong enough to master. Yet this fundamental conservatism is compounded by the injustice of Troyat's attack on existentialism in some of its specific manifestations. Thuillier himself is a caricature, the word "tuile" denoting bad luck in popular speech,[2] and, when he is allowed to speak, he presents, not a clear exposé of existentialist thought, but a "curious amalgam of the ideas of Sartre and Nietzsche,"[3] deliberately set up in order to be demolished. Instead of a reasoned critique of Thuillier's position, Troyat enters into an *ad hominem* attack, in which he emphasizes the philosopher's unkempt appearance, his liking for cheap restaurants, and his indifference to Etienne's problems when he is enjoying himself in the company of friends. Further, Troyat amplifies this line of criticism by evoking the superficial aspects of the existentialist heyday in Saint Germain-des-Près, in which the serious intellectual preoccupations of the movement become subordinated to a popular image of jazz, nightclubs, and sexual promiscuity. In this respect, Troyat's novel remains on the same level as the popular press which, as Francis Jeanson records, attributed any adolescent disorder to "des douleurs existentialistes"[4] ("existentialist heartaches").

Ironically, *La Tête sur les épaules* is by no means as removed from existentialist preoccupations as the criticism of Thuillier would indicate. The philosopher's refusal to offer advice to Etienne is entirely consistent with Sartre's position in his, admittedly overstated, *L'Existentialisme est un humanisme,*[5] and it has the entirely Sartrean effect of forcing Etienne to seek his own solution. His subsequent rejection of the false mantle of his father and his assumption of a mature role in a new family comprised of Marion and Maxime Joubert constitute a vital step toward authenticity and "l'âge de raison," in the same way that Jacques Sorbier's final escape from the false persona of Georges Galard is a defeat of "mauvaise foi." What is important, however, is that, while the Sartrean search for authenticity leads almost automatically to a break with the conventions of bourgeois society, the evolution of Etienne Martin, like that of the *Bildungsroman,* is in the opposite direction, toward a just appreciation of the values of love, the family, and established order. In this evolution the role of Joubert is critical, to the extent that he becomes the *raisonneur* in the novel, the expression of the author's faith in a middle way between intellectuality and love. For Joubert, the cultivated businessman, who can feel at ease in the philosophy of Schopenhauer, Rousseau, and Hegel, as well as running a successful commercial enterprise, is Troyat's first expression of the ideal combination of the world of ideas and the world of practical existence.

It is he who is the true architect of the surrender of Etienne's bogus existentialism to the incontrovertible happiness of Marion. *La Tête sur les épaules* has been one of Troyat's most successful novels. Despite its success, however, it is important to emphasize the novel's shortcomings. Troyat is not at ease in the novel of ideas, precisely because that genre, from Malraux onward, demands the minimizing of the psychology of the characters in favor of the abstract concepts they express and in whose world they have their being. The concentration upon Etienne Martin as an adolescent, with added psychological tensions, serves to produce a hybrid novel, in which the depiction and consideration of ideas are too often reduced to caricature. In the case of Troyat, the fiction of ideas lends itself much more to the *romans-fleuves*, in which there is ample space for abstract preoccupation within the context of fully drawn characters. It is not an attempt which he makes again in his short fiction.

La Neige en deuil

Troyat's next novel, which appeared in 1952, is one of his best-known works and achieved a wide English-speaking audience with the Dmytryk film version, *The Mountain,* which somewhat improbably cast Spencer Tracy as the Alpine guide Isaïe.[6] In comparison with the previous short fiction, it appears to constitute a major departure: no longer is it concerned with the problems of adolescence; it moves from the claustrophobic interiors of *Le Vivier* and *L'Araigne* to the rarified external world, as it moves from the ill-defined Parisian settings to the French Alps. At the same time, the innovatory aspects of *La Neige en deuil* are largely superficial and Troyat's interest remains fixed upon the same psychological tensions which inform the other novels.

The work concerns the fifty-year-old Isaïe Vaudagne, who has once been a great Alpine guide but whose career was cut short when bad luck struck on two occasions, causing the loss of his clients and injuring him so badly that his mental faculties are permanently impaired and he is reduced to an almost childlike state. He lives with his younger brother Marcellin, who contrasts with Isaïe's innocence in his greed, cynicism, and brutality and who dominates him by his constant threat to move to the city. This long-standing tension between the two brothers reaches its crisis when an airliner, on its way from India, crashes on the mountaintop above the village. Marcellin, hearing that the plane was carrying a cargo of precious stones, conceives the idea of climbing secretly to the summit and robbing the wreck. In order to do this, he needs the help of Isaïe, and blackmails him into leading the climb with renewed threats that he will leave for the city and undertake the expedition alone. As they plan their ascent, and as they move up the mountain, Isaïe recovers his old skills and a new moral superiority, to the extent that he can view Marcellin dispassionately as a greedy coward. Once on the summit, he abandons his brother to his looting, and looks to see if he can help any of the victims. Only one, a young Indian woman, is still alive, and Isaïe prepares to carry her down to the village, brutally repulsing Marcellin's attempts to stop him and leaving his brother to die on the mountain. The novel ends with Isaïe carrying the woman into his cottage, unaware that she has died during the descent.

In his comments on the novel, Troyat recalls, in *Un si long chemin,* that 'it was a combination of two preoccupations, "cette brusque flambée de haine d'un être bon et humble contre un frère qui l'écrasait jusque-là par son intelligence" ("that brief blaze of hatred of a good and humble man for a brother who, until then, had dominated him with his intelligence," 146), and a factual event, the crash of the Indian airliner, the *Malabar Princess,* on the slopes of Mont Blanc in November 1950. In *Un si long chemin* he describes how one night the two elements of the novel fused together in his mind in their entirety, so that, in a sort of dream, he conceived the whole narrative, from episode to episode. Significantly, the novel appeared to him in black and white, a fact which led him to maintain an austere narrative with minimal picturesque elements.[7] Nevertheless, some documentation was necessary, and Troyat set off to Chamonix with his wife, who knew the area well, to consult an ex-guide Luc Tournier, who showed him the geographical setting and provided technical details. In spite of this realist documentation, however, Troyat insists on the primacy of the psychological elements, "Qu'on ne s'avise surtout pas de considérer *La Neige en deuil* comme un roman inspiré par l'alpinisme et destiné à glorifier la technique hasardeuse d'un guide. Mon propos, dans cette affaire, n'a pas été d'animer quelques personnages passe-partout pour servir de prétexte à la description d'une première hivernale. Je me suis interdit de sacrifier la psychologie de mes héros au récit de l'ascension qu'ils ont entreprise"[8] ("Do not consider *La Neige en deuil* as a novel inspired by climbing and aimed at the glorification of the dangerous technique of a guide. In this novel, my aim was not to create one or two all-purpose characters as a pretext for the description of a first ascent. I refused to sacrifice the psychology of my heroes to the story of their climb"), and concludes, "L'essentiel, dans *La Neige en deuil,* ce n'est pas la neige, c'est le deuil" ("In *La Neige en deuil,* the main thing is not the snow, but the mourning," 147).

The real interest of the novel, therefore, lies in the conflict between the two brothers, Isaïe and Marcellin, a preoccupation which places *La Neige en deuil* in the mainstream of Troyat's short fiction. The name of the hero, however, together with the austere and elemental setting, places the novel in a general mythical context in which biblical struggles between brothers, Cain and Abel, Jacob and Esau, Joseph, are echoed. At the same time, in the childlike perception and goodness of Isaïe, and the deforming intelligence of Marcellin, Troyat makes use of a Christian literary tradition most strikingly expressed in Dostoevski's *The Idiot.* In the construction of his characters, Troyat employs a quite complicated procedure. As W. D. Howarth points out in his introduction to the novel, Isaïe's accident, which makes him become "as a child," inverts his relationship with Marcellin who becomes a father figure, dominating and leading him on.[9] This inversion produces both positive and negative effects: it establishes Isaïe's moral superiority over his brother, but at the same time places him in the same stultifying situation of dependency and fear which inhibits Etienne Martin. Throughout the first part of the novel, Isaïe is totally subjected to the emotional blackmail of Marcellin, a blackmail which obliges him to undertake an expedition which he finds physically frightening and morally repugnant.

Ironically for Marcellin, the climb redresses the inversion: Isaïe rediscovers his old skill as a climber and, with that, his role, literally, as a guide, the superiority of the leader. The success of the climb permits him to finally escape his psychological dependency on Marcellin and assert his belief in moral absolutes over the degeneracy of his brother. In this way, the novel becomes a triumph of moral decency and psychological normality. Nevertheless, the ambiguity of the ending is disturbing. Isaïe's heroic self-assertion against Marcellin does not lead to the successful rescue of the Indian woman but to the descent of her corpse, a corpse which Isaïe deludedly believes to be still alive. That the novel should end with a death and the retreat of the hero into his previous childlike world calls into question any optimistic interpretation. In the same way that Dostoevski's Prince Mishkin returns to madness after the death of Nastasia Philipovna, Isaïe returns to conversation with his animals, the only beings who do not possess the malevolence of the world. The novel therefore concludes on a more somber note than *La Tête sur les épaules* and seems to lack even the modest confidence in humanity expressed by Bourdieu in *Le Signe du taureau*. As Howarth emphasizes, it is on physical, not theoretical terms that Isaïe triumphs over Marcellin, and his horror at his brother's plan to rob the dead is translated into a violent physical attack: the assertion of humanity proves fragile indeed, and, ultimately, only temporary.

Une Extrême amitié

La Neige en deuil achieves an admirable simplicity of narration, mainly by being set in such a geographically isolated position. In that way, its apparent novelty marks the final stage in a line of fiction running from *Faux Jour* onward, where the psychological drama of dependency and domination can ultimately be renewed only by a radical change of location. It is perhaps this sense of having exhausted the genre which accounts for the fact that there is a gap of eleven years between *La Neige en deuil* and the next short novel, *Une Extrême amitié* (1963), a gap which Troyat himself explains by his concentration on the *romans-fleuves,* but which indicates a more general technical uncertainty.

Une Extême amitié deals with a couple, Jean Heurtelot, an eminent medical researcher with the CNRS, and his wife, Madeleine, who is a professional translator from English, who go to spend their fifteenth wedding anniversary in the south of France. There, they unexpectedly meet an old school friend of Jean's, Bernard, who had introduced him to his first wife, Muriel, and had broken with him after warning him not to marry, seventeen years previously. Jean is by no means pleased to renew acquaintance with Bernard, but agrees to visit a nightclub with him and his young mistress, Corinne. Back in Paris, however, Jean's initial reluctance reverts to the original hero-worship, and he copies Bernard in everything, even attending the same physical-training sessions as his idol and sleeping, just once, with Corinne because she has been Bernard's mistress. Rapidly,

Jean and Madeleine become drawn into Bernard's world, dining with him regularly and visiting his new country house, La Roncière. It is through this house that the puzzling denouement occurs: Jean is called from his laboratory one day to be informed that Madeleine and Bernard have been killed in a road accident on the way back from La Roncière, and the novel closes leaving Jean with the question of whether the car journey was quite innocent or whether Bernard and Madeleine were lovers.

In *Un si long chemin* Troyat describes the novel as the story of "la destruction du présent par le passé" "the destruction of the present by the past," (185–86), a comment which highlights the vulnerability of the present and the almost ghostlike role of Bernard who reemerges from the past to haunt Jean and control him, as Georges Galard controls Sorbier. In this context, it is significant that Troyat once again explores the relationship of dependency of a weak character on a strong one and provides a further study of one of his favorite types, the weak male. In the case of Jean Heurtelot, the weakness and the dependency achieve unhealthy proportions. Jean's first wife Muriel had been Bernard's mistress before Jean married her, a fact which announces precisely the only attraction of Corinne. Jean's attempt is to copy Bernard in all ways until he adopts Bernard's persona and actually becomes his idol: hence his participation in physical training, his fad of pipe smoking. It is this unhealthy identification with Bernard which constitutes the unusual extremity of the relationship. Ironically, it is an attempt at identification which perverts Jean's character and masks his very real prestige as a medical researcher. In this context, the novel tends to reflect the relationship between Duhamel's narrator, the scientist Laurent Pasquier, and his ebullient businessman brother, Joseph, in which the scientific achievements of the former fade in comparison with the sheer dynamism and physical force of the latter.

The destruction of the present is rendered permanent by the deaths of Bernard and Madeleine and the query that hangs tantalizingly over their relationship. In this respect, Troyat creates a powerfully ironic ending in which Jean, whose sole ambition has been identification with Bernard, is forever excluded from the relationship between his hero and Madeleine. Similarly, Troyat is careful to provide Jean with insufficient evidence concerning the reasons for the final journey, so that he remains in a state of ignorance and indecision which assumes almost tragic proportions. Nevertheless, the novel itself provides ample material pointing toward an affair between Bernard and Madeleine. The fact that they die in a car accident merely consecrates their shared fascination for automobiles, an enthusiasm from which Jean, a nondriver, is excluded. The careful description of the first meeting between the two couples, while dwelling on Jean's embarrassment and distaste, also shows Madeleine's instinctive liking for Bernard and her perceptive observation that Bernard and Corinne are overacting the role of a happy couple. The most subtle indication of a possible relationship between Bernard and Madeleine is given when, after a long silence, the businessman invites the Heurtelots for a weekend at La Roncière, a visit during which they confidently expect to meet his new mistress. Both are surprised, therefore, to find Bernard alone: yet, if there were an affair between Bernard and Madeleine, then the absent mistress would be present, and it would be Jean who is alone, and not Bernard. With this carefully constructed doubt which destroys Jean's faith in the past relationship with his wife, Troyat ends powerfully at the point where Simenon chooses to begin his exploration, in *Les Innocents* (1972).

In the structuring of the narrative, Troyat has shown considerable skill. The brief affair between Jean and Corinne, for example, is not merely a faithful reflection of the original marriage with Bernard's other mistress, Muriel, but serves to divert the reader from the expected inevitability of an affair between Bernard and Madeleine. At the same time, the novel presents serious technical problems. In his interview with Troyat, Gilbert Ganne refers to the charges made when the work was published that it was exploiting the success of Françoise Sagan.[10] As Troyat himself replies, such charges are hardly fair if they are based on social settings and geographical locations which are common property. Nevertheless, the criticism highlights a weakness in the novel in its use of a stereotyped character, the bronzed, handsome, mature, rich Bernard, and a stereotyped setting in which the trappings of wealth, fast cars, luxurious apartments, and chic restaurants constitute an easy exoticism. More serious are the problems of the narrative itself. The very subject matter of the novel, the invasion of the present by the past, necessarily invites the technical difficulties of introducing past experience into the present relationship between Jean and Bernard, and these difficulties are not successfully surmounted. One procedure which Troyat employs looks forward to the character Klim, in *Les*

Héritiers de l'avenir: the introduction into the text of Jean's boyhood diary, showing his subservience, even at lycée, to Bernard. This technique works tolerably well, except for the fact that its use is so isolated that it tends to jar with the rest of the narrative. Less successful is the use of flashback within the text, as in the scene in the restaurant in the south, where Troyat cuts cinematographically from the present to Jean's past. Thus, as the waiters prepare a complicated dish at the table, "Un garçon subalterne suivait la cérémonie, l'oeil vitreux de respect. Il pouvait être dix heures du soir. Jean travaillait chez lui sur un article que le professeur Landier lui avait demandé d'écrire. Coup de sonnette à la porte"[11] ("an assistant waiter followed the ceremony, his eyes glazed with respect. It must be about ten o'clock. Jean was working at home on an article which Professor Landier had asked him to write. The doorbell rang. . . ."). The overuse of this technique becomes unhelpful and tends to impede the narrative without clearly conveying the intended relationship of present to past. Rather than being a procedure of the *nouveau roman,* as Ganne sees it, it resembles the irritating cross-cutting in mid-sentence that does nothing to enhance Sartre's *Le Sursis.*

Troyat's return to the short novel after a period of ten years is not, therefore, a total success and does not resolve the problem of the genre's limitations. However impressive the dilemma at the end of the novel, Jean's dependency on Bernard and his inability to escape from the past constitute no real thematic progression on the wartime novels, *Le Mort saisit le vif* and *Le Signe du taureau.* More disturbingly, the change of setting leads to a use of stereotypes, and attempts at stylistic innovation become too often disruptive. It is perhaps for these reasons that there is a further gap of nine years before the next short novel, a work which heads a whole series in which Troyat restorès narrative simplicity and asserts the primacy of the story.

France in the 1970s

Between 1972 and 1977 Troyat wrote three short novels set in contemporary Paris in which he returns to his interwar themes of "rêve" contrasted with "réalité" and the struggle for domestic domination. In the first of these, *La Pierre, la feuille et les ciseaux* (The stone, the paper, and the scissors), Troyat uses the "ménage à trois"

subject hinted at in *Une Extrême amitié,* concentrating this time on
a main character who is a homosexual, a fact which earned him
some adverse criticism when the novel appeared. André, a painter,
is supervising the decoration of a friend's house in Fayence, near
Grasse, when he meets Frédéric, a charismatic young vagabond.
When André has returned to his apartment in the rue Saint-Honoré,
Frédéric arrives unexpectedly and moves in, displacing André's lover
Constantine. The relationship is complicated by Frédéric falling in
love with André's best woman friend, Sabine, and making her pregnant. The three adults and the child live in uneasy proximity in
André's apartment until Frédéric is lured to America by Richter,
André's art dealer. Sabine decides to follow Frédéric, leaving the
baby, Léon, with the ever-accommodating André. Eventually, however, it becomes clear that neither parent will return, and the novel
ends with André setting out to leave Léon with his sister in the
same way that he gave her all his stray pets as a child.

The title of the novel comes from the children's game in which
the hands of the two players must spontaneously make shapes.
Depending on the choice, the players win points: the paper will
win over the stone, but will lose to the scissors which, in turn, will
break on the stone. The title therefore becomes a powerful image
of the "ménage à trois" in which each of the participants is striving
for domination but continually seeing his efforts canceled out. Yet,
in this emotional game not all the characters are equal, and the
action is orchestrated by the deceptively weak painter, André. On
one level, André is yet another of the weak male characters who
people Troyat's novels, like Jean Heurtelot or Patrice, in *Tendre et
violente Elizabeth.* More profoundly, however, his role is the same as
that of Guillaume in *Faux Jour,* that of a magician who denies and
transforms reality. In his characterization, Troyat follows a reduc-
tively determinist psychology and views André as the inevitable son
of a mother who "avait toujours fermé la porte à la vie réelle"[12]
("had always closed the door on real life"). Thus, André's profession
as a painter and, particularly, as an interior decorator, conveys his
transforming role, a role accentuated by his mania for renaming
those around him so that they become part of his dreamworld:
Frédéric becomes Aurélio; the romantically named Coriandre, his
sister, has in reality the more banal name of Alice. Through this
elegant stage managing and his subtle insinuation into the emotional
lives of his companions, the weak André becomes a figure of some

power. Ultimately, however, he is still vulnerable to the forces which threaten all of Troyat's dreamers: the reality principle cannot be disguised forever; Frédéric shakes off the name Aurélio and reasserts his autonomy. Yet, in this inevitable assault by reality, André has one refuge which permits him to remain in a childlike world of dreams: his sister, to whom he abandons the baby who is the result of his dream existence, just as a child will reject a pet in which it has lost interest.

The portrait of André, though irritating at times in its irresponsibility, is sympathetic and well drawn. In the case of Frédéric-Aurélio, however, Troyat has been unable to escape the stereotypes which mar *Une Extrême amitié*. Frédéric appears too heavily and too blatantly as the "free spirit," overturning convention and relying on a morality whose sole base is hedonism. Not only is this a tedious transposition of the cults of the late 1960s, it is also psychologically unconvincing as the larger-than-life bohemian becomes the sharp businessman overnight. What interests Troyat in Frédéric, however, is his amoral hedonistic philosophy in which any act is justified as long as it brings pleasure. This connects with Troyat's meditations on the cynical German teacher, Christian Walter, in *Tendre et violente Elizabeth,* in which, again, the amorality proves worrying and threatening. The exaggerated attractiveness of characters like Christian and Frédéric, with their consequently repugnant philosophy, testify to a continuing moral conservatism which informs Troyat's fiction, in which the family, even André's bizarre household, is not to be lightly overturned.

If Troyat returns to his proccupations with reality in *La Pierre, la feuille et les ciseaux,* in his next novel, *Anne Prédaille* (1973), he exploits his other major theme of the 1930s, the domination, within a family, of the weak by the strong. The novel is constructed around the question raised in *Un si long chemin:* "A quel moment l'altruisme se transforme-t-il en tyrannie?" ("At what point is altruism turned into tyranny?" 220). The heroine, Anne, is the only, divorced daughter of Pierre and Emilienne Prédaille. At the age of thirty she is already the head of the art section of a publishing company and is the dominant figure in her family, her father being unemployed and her mother terminally ill. Faced with the intolerable pain suffered by Emilienne, she has the strength to administer a fatal overdose, a strength rendered ambiguous by the fact that she has already embarked upon an affair with a young bohemian, Laurent, whom she has permitted to live in the family's *chambre de bonne*. After the death of Mily, Troyat charts the rise to absolute power of Anne: she stifles the life of her father, destroying his attempts to rehabilitate himself by marrying the niece of his bookseller, Hélène, and drives the weak Laurent to despair with her demands that he work in the same company as herself, so that he finally commits suicide. The novel ends with Anne's promotion, Laurent's death, and the reduction of her father to a state of premature senility.

Anne Prédaille is one of Troyat's most successful short novels. It avoids the feyness of *La Pierre, la feuille et les ciseaux* and, unlike *La Neige en deuil*, contains no extraneous exotic elements which clash with the main body of the narrative. At the same time, that narration is carefully controlled without being self-consciously experimental, as in the case of *Une Extrême amitié*. What Troyat accomplishes admirably is a subtle manipulation of the reader in the course of the novel from initial admiration and sympathy for Anne to condemnation of her tyranny, with a consequent realization of Laurent's weakness and her father's need for affection. In this way Troyat achieves something often absent from his short fiction, the evolution of his characters and his reader's reactions, rather than the inexorable playing out of a preestablished psychological drama. This evolution is held together by a carefully constructed parallelism which heightens the injustice of Anne's rise to power. Her father, after a decent interval following his wife's death, takes a younger mistress and is punished for it; Anne, even during Mily's illness, takes a younger lover and contrives to destroy both him and her father.

The weakest part of the novel is that which concerns Laurent, one of the amoral bohemians who form a constant preoccupation in these three novels of the 1970s. The problem is that Troyat confers exaggerated importance on the post-1968 generation, to the extent that his fictional representatives of this age group become stereotypes. Laurent continues the work of Frédéric-Aurelio, and looks forward to Paul Lecapellet in *Le Front dans les nuages (Head in the Clouds)*, but whereas Frédéric irritates by his self-confidence and easy domination of those around him, Laurent annoys by his innate weakness and his growing dependency on Anne. His comment at the beginning of the novel, "Je suis ce qu'on appelle un raté"[13] ("I am what is known as a raté"), goes far deeper than a proclamation of social *contestation* and indicates his true emotional frailty. Similarly, Troyat's later description, "Il ressemblait à un gitan malchanceux" ("He looked like a Gypsy down on his luck," 220), points the contrast with that successful gypsy, Frédéric, and announces Laurent's imminent death.

If the inclusion of the portrait of Laurent constitutes a weakness, however, the other two actors in this "ménage à trois" are admirably drawn. Troyat sympathetically follows Pierre's progress from incompetence in the household, through total prostration at the death of Mily, to rediscovery of his self-esteem in his relationship with Hélène and his managership of the antiquarian bookshop. His renewed professional and emotional self-confidence are shattered irreversibly by Anne's refusal to countenance a remarriage and her curt dismissal of Hélène, and in this intervention by Anne, Troyat establishes a more complex motivation than that which prompts similar actions in L'Araigne. Like Gérard Fonsèque, Anne wants sole domination of the household; yet, whereas Gérard's attempt to dictate is founded on his psychological dependency on his dead mother and her representatives, his sisters, that of Anne is the result of a gradual progression from competence to tyranny, a progression which she cannot totally control. It is significant that she finds Laurent work in a subordinate position in her own publishing house, so that he is both emotionally and professionally inferior, a fact signified by his occupation of the chambre de bonne, where he is, literally, a servant. This desire to manage others, to know what is better for them, like Gérard, is part of her domination of Pierre, but it is subtly combined with other elements: Pierre's remarriage would precipitate a change in Anne's role in the apartment and would either force her to marry Laurent or leave her alone and expose her weakness; similarly, a remarriage would constitute a murder of Mily's memory, which reminds Anne unpleasantly of her physical murder of her mother. In addition, the parallel between Anne and her father is maintained by the fact that Anne, as a divorcee, is faced by the problem of remarriage herself, and her emotional inability to take that step leads her to deny her father's happiness.

In the portrait of Anne, Troyat has produced one of his most convincing and powerful "monstres," yet one who is psychologically complex and whose professional and domestic strength conceal an emotional weakness. This is conveyed by a single effective image: constant reference is made to the way in which Pierre and Anne have the habit of drinking white wine while Laurent, when he joins them, drinks only water. Not only does this indicate Laurent's

weakness and exclusion from the family group, it also places Pierre
and Anne together so that they reflect each other and come to share
the same qualities. The white wine constitutes the only visible
dependency that Anne possesses, but it indicates that her evolution
will go uncontrollably beyond domination to the same dependency
and need for affection that she despises in her father.

The subject of the "ménage à trois" and the relationship between
a dominant professional woman and a dreamer is continued in *Le
Front dans les nuages* (1977). The central character is Marguerite
Cassoyeur, aged fifty-five, a Russian specialist now working on the
biography of the poet and soldier Denis Davidoff. She shares her
apartment in the rue de l'Université with Germaine Taff, a dominant
businesswoman of the same age. Their calm spinsterish life together
is disrupted when they decide to advertise for a lodger and are
confronted by Paul Lecapellet, a young and irresponsible dreamer,
the descendant of Frédéric and Laurent, who gradually insinuates
himself into the apartment and refuses to leave. The fantasy world
which he represents and conjures up fascinates the poetic Marguerite,
but is perceived accurately by Germaine as a serious threat. Used
to dominating Marguerite, she insists upon Paul's departure, but
meets unexpected opposition. Her position is further weakened when
she suffers a heart attack and is forced to spend weeks in hospital,
while the apartment is given over to fantasy and even her own room
is redecorated. Her return as a petulant invalid threatens to destroy
the dreamworld of Marguerite and Paul, and they contrive to murder
her by inducing another heart attack after a gargantuan meal which
they know she will be unable to resist. Yet, with the death of
Germaine an essential element is missing from Marguerite's life, an
element restored when Paul finds a new lodger, a dominant, fifty-
year-old beautician.

Compared with *Anne Prédaille, Le Front dans les nuages* is a slighter
work, though it continues to exploit material by now familiar in
Troyat's fiction. The young interloper, Paul, is less substantial than
Frédéric or Laurent, and so becomes more credible and able to fulfill
his role of authentic purveyor of the dream life, a role which res-
urrects the positive elements of Guillaume, in *Faux Jour*. Yet the
real interest of the novel lies in the complex character of the biographer, Marguerite who, similarly, draws together many elements
present in the previous novels. Thus, she follows Gérard Fonsèque
in attributing to the apartment a positive protective and comforting

role. Also, in her apparent subservience to the sensitive and dominant Germaine, she reflects the dependency of Philippe on Madame Chasseglin, in *Le Vivier*. She is more complex, however, than either Gérard or Philippe in that, by the end of the novel, she has achieved equilibrium between two demands: the need for comfort, protection, subservience, as well as a need for escape, freedom, and dreams. Marguerite may enjoy having her head in the clouds, she also desperately requires the certainty of feeling her feet on the ground. Yet, in this successful search for equilibrium, it is Marguerite, and not Paul or Germaine, who occupies the center of the stage and who allows the action to be manipulated in her interests. In this indirect control of events, she comes to resemble the dreamer André of *La Pierre, la feuille et les ciseaux*.

Troyat's three French novels of the 1970s, therefore, do not extend his thematic range much beyond that of his interwar fiction. He still concentrates upon the relationship between dominance and subservience in a narrow domestic setting and upon the acceptability of the dreamworld in the context of day-to-day existence, a concentration by no means disguised by superficial changes in setting. Nor does Troyat arrive at any positive conclusion. The dreamworld of André or Marguerite is only possible because their lives are sheltered from the exterior by financial independence and intermediaries among their entourage. In the real world, Anne Prédaille's search for success becomes a generalized will to power which destroys those around her and threatens obliquely to destroy her too. The only new element, the presence in the novels of the young antisocial dreamer, a reflection of the disenchanted youth of the 1960s, serves merely to reinforce the main characters in choices they have already, if sometimes unconsciously, taken.

Russia in the Eighteenth Century

In the late 1970s, while still completing the Parisian series of novels, Troyat produced two works which, in their subject matter and their setting, constitute a radical break with the rest of his short fiction. All of the short novels, from *Faux Jour* to *Le Front dans les nuages,* are set in contemporary France and, with the exception of *La Neige en deuil,* concentrate on claustrophobic interior settings which generate of themselves the thematic structures of dominance-subservience and dream-reality. In *Grimbosq* (1976) and *Le Prisonnier*

No. 1, (1978), however, Troyat chooses the setting of eighteenth-century Russia, with the use of factual historical characters, and seeks to renew the short novel form by injecting into it material and preoccupations used previously only in the *romans-fleuves*.

Grimbosq is set in St. Petersburg in the last years of the reign of Peter the Great, from 1721 to 1725. Etienne Grimbosq, a French architect, is invited, with his wife Adrienne and his daughter Louison, to Russia to construct a palace for the Court Chamberlain, Romachkine. In spite of his dislike of the barbarity of Peter's court and his wife's premonitions, he allows himself to be retained in St. Petersburg on completion of the palace in order to build the church of Saint-Antipe. As the church rises, Grimbosq's own life collapses: his wife has an affair with Romachkine and a child by him; his daughter dies, a death which so totally demoralizes Adrienne that she sinks into a life of debauchery and is murdered by a sailor. Grimbosq, however, remains indifferent, consumed by a passion for his church. Yet the building is unable to resist the River Neva and it begins to subside, with cracks appearing in the walls. The architect is able to convince Peter that he should carry on, but with the death of the emperor and the accession of his wife Catherine, he loses his influence at court and his project is terminated. The novel ends with Grimbosq going mad and being shipped back to France with his illegitimate son as his church is demolished in the background.

The work is an historical novel to the extent that it is remarkably accurately documented on the construction of St. Petersburg. Indeed, it was this initial documentation which served as the impetus and the basis for the 1979 biography of Peter the Great. This raises the question, however, of the status of the novel as a whole, whether it constitutes the continuation of the short "roman intime" in an exotic historical setting, or whether it has been able to go further and blend the psychological drama of the characters with the broader historical tragedy of Peter himself so as to produce a new tone in the short fiction. Clearly, beneath the technical detail of the growth of the new Russian capital and the exotic evocation of the gaudy barbarity of the imperial court, the domestic tensions between Grimbosq and Adrienne have familiar features. Once again, Troyat chooses to portray an inherently weak man, who marries a perceptive and strong woman, and unthinkingly places his family at the mercy of dangerous forces by devoting himself to an obsession.

Grimbosq's decision to go to Russia and, more important, to remain there, has the same unforseen tragic results as Vautier's launching of his son on a theatrical career. His neglect of his wife for his work and his lack of awareness of the dangers represented by surrounding predatory men has the same consequences as Jean's blinding self-obsession in *Une Extrême amitié.* Similarly, the causes of the tragedy lie in Grimbosq's childlike devotion to his dream. Adrienne comments, half-affectionately, half-bitterly, "Cher Etienne, tu es un enfant. Il ne faut pas te déranger dans ton jeu de cubes!"[14] ("Dear Etienne, you are a child. You must not be disturbed while you are playing with your bricks!"), and the child's game removes him so far from reality that he finaly faces the accusation of Peter's successor, Catherine I, "Vous avez rêvé, rêvé, rêvé, le front dans les nuages" ("You have been dreaming, with your head in the clouds," 303).

The banal domestic crisis, however, by which an intelligent wife resents being placed at risk by a childishly unthinking husband and is unfaithful to him, a situation reminiscent of Godard's film *Le Mépris,* is given weight and depth by the historical dimensions of the novel. The story appears to be calqued on Pushkin's *The Bronze Horseman,* discussed by Troyat in his biography of the poet, in which a young inhabitant of St. Petersburg rails against the pride of the city's founder which has led him to establish a capital on the uncontrollable Neva, which bursts its banks and drowns his fiancée. In the same way, the flooding of the city becomes a recurrent motif in *Grimbosq* and signifies the destruction of the architect's marriage, as the result of a tyrant's ambition. Grimbosq and his family are prisoners in the court which constitutes Peter's *vivier,* and are unable to escape. At the same time, as Troyat himself points out in *Un si long chemin,* the interest moves to the character of the czar himself: "le roman de Grimbosq devenait le roman de Grimbosq et de Pierre le Grand. Au lieu d'un personnage central, j'en avais deux. L'un bâtissait une église et l'autre un empire" ("the novel of Grimbosq became the novel of Grimbosq and Peter the Great. Instead of one central character, I had two. One was building a church, the other an empire," 228–29). The church of Saint-Antipe becomes the symbol of Peter's new Russia: it has a European exterior, but the interior is Russian, in the same way that the new Russia looked toward the West while remaining irredeemably Slavic at heart. It is for this reason that the edifice is cracked: the novel describes the

downfall of Peter's grandiose ambition to build a modern Russia in
one generation through the way in which the architect overreaches
himself. The destinies of Peter the Great and Grimbosq thus become linked
and reflect each other. Significantly, it is as they both decline that
they develop a close affinity: Grimbosq, betrayed by his wife, watches
his life's work collapse; the czar, who has just discovered Catherine's
infidelity, becomes a sick and lonely figure beset by doubts, a figure
who, curiously, has a pathos lacking in Troyat's nonfictional portrait
in *Pierre le Grand*. In this parallel between the architect and his
master, Troyat expresses a deep historical fatalism which informs
the *romans-fleuves*. Czar and commoner share the same fate: there is
no permanency in great works; the church is demolished, Peter's
work is undone by his successors; the tide of history washes over
great and small alike. The leitmotiv of the novel cycles, "Qu'allons-
nous devenir?" ("What is to become of us?" 164), which expresses
a helpless grief at the march of unalterable events, is repeated here
by Adrienne, but no character in the novel is immune. What dominates is a sense of metaphysical evil which Peter the Great has
conjured up but which has now escaped his control and which is
symbolized by the river. Troyat writes of Grimbosq at the end of
the novel: "Il existait entre la Néva et lui une relation mystérieuse,
surnaturelle, comme il en existe parfois entre les êtres. Cette eau
était maléfique. Elle avait miné le sol, elle avait miné sa vie" ("Between the Neva and him there was a mysterious, supernatural relationship, as there is sometimes between people. This water was
evil. It had undermined the soil, it had undermined his life," 307).
The novel thus ends with a return to the satanic world of the short
stories.

Grimbosq marks a successful departure from the traditional world
of Troyat's short fiction. In spite of the persistence of the same
psychological tensions and the commercial attractiveness of the exotic Russian decor, the novel achieves stature as a portrait of obsession, ambition, and historical fragility. In comparison, a similar
use of eighteenth-century Russian material in *Le Prisonnier No. 1* is
less fruitful because the historical grandeur of Grimbosq and Peter
is subordinated to the demands of plot, restrained in its turn by
the conditions of historical accuracy. Nevertheless, it achieves considerable power. It is set in the early years of the reign of Catherine
the Great and is built upon the factual events surrounding the

attempt to replace Catherine by the mad Czar Ivan VI, held prisoner in the Schlüsselburg Fortress, the "Prisoner No. 1" of the title. The central character, the factual Basile Mirovitch, is a poor junior officer whose family has been in disgrace since the Mazeppa uprising against Peter the Great. In an attempt to gain redress, he is received by the empress's favorite, Grégoire Orlov, who agrees only to find him a posting nearer the capital. As a mark of Orlov's black humor, this posting proves to be to the guard of the Schlüsselburg fortress and constitutes almost an exile in itself. At first embittered by his failure with Orlov, Mirovitch gradually falls under the spell of the fortress in the middle of its calm lake and even requests supplementary guard duty so that he may spend more time there. It is by knowing the castle and the permanent guard better than his colleagues that he becomes aware of the existence of "le Prisonnier No. 1," the legendary mad Czar Ivan VI. It is at this point that Basile's fascination with the fortress, his veneration of Ivan, his bitterness at his treatment by Catherine's favorite, and his desire for wealth and success all combine to shape in his mind the plot to release the mad czar and set him in the place of the overthrown empress. This plan rapidly becomes an obsession, drawing him away from his love for Aglaé Nossov, the daughter of a rich political exile, and is doomed to failure: as Basile and his troops storm the fortress, the czar is murdered by his guards on Catherine's instructions. Basile is captured and finally executed, despite Aglaé's moving appeal to the empress herself.

The novel's power lies in the way in which Basile grows in stature as the plot against Catherine progresses. Troyat emphasizes the pettiness of his original ambition and the narrowness of his mind. Writing of this at the beginning of the novel, he comments, "Il avait l'esprit sérieux, lourd, géométrique. La pauvreté ne dispose pas à la fantaisie"[15] ("His mind was serious, heavy, geometrical. Poverty does not lend itself to imagination"), and he describes Basile's arrival at the reception where he he is to meet Orlov in terms which recall Balzac's characterization of Rastignac: "Il les détestait et il les enviait. Il leur déclarait la guerre et, dans le même temps, il se sentait prêt à toutes les bassesses pour être accepté dans leur confrerie" ("He hated them and he envied them. He declared war on them and, at the same time, he felt capable of any self-abasement in order to be accepted into their number," 37). The mystifying power of the castle of Schlüsselburg, which becomes an

ever-present character in its own right, confers upon him the quality
of imagination which he has previously lacked and leads him to an
understanding of the significance of Ivan VI which, infused with
religious mysticism, becomes an obsession, in the same way that
the construction of the church of Saint-Antipe dominates and destroys Grimbosq. The obsession leads Basile to identify, first, with
the rebel Cossak, the source of his family's misfortunes, then with
Ivan himself: both are victims of Catherine the Great, both are
imprisoned in the fortress of Schlüsselburg. The parallel continues,
of course, in ways that Basile is unable to see: his obsession comes
to resemble Ivan's madness; both men die as victims of the plot.
Finally, Basile, the penniless young officer, actually becomes Ivan
as he enters legend. The reign of Catherine had been threatened at
the outset by popular rumors that her dead husband Peter and Czar
Ivan were really alive and would return to overthrow the usurper.
The novel closes with the boatmen gliding past Schlüsselburg and
talking of Basile in the same terms as they talked of Ivan and Peter:
"En vérité, Basile Mirovitch n'est pas mort . . ." ("In fact, Basile
Mirovitch is not dead . . .," 288–89).

Troyat is clear, however, that, if Basile has risen from petty
ambition to legendary status, he has done so by following an absolute
aim which is ultimately death oriented. In the person of Aglaé, he
provides a powerful representative of the value of "bonheur" who,
in the way in which she fights for Basile's life, which he no longer
wants, resembles not so much the theatrical romanticism of Stendhal's Mathilde de la Mole in Le Rouge et le noir, as the practical
assertion of a woman's right to her husband found in Amélie in Les
Semailles et les moissons, and in Sophie in La Lumière des justes. Troyat
remains consistent in distrusting historical action and in maintaining
the values of the couple and the family against the pursuit of the
absolute.

The novel is tightly constructed. An example of this is the point
where Aglaé, thinking of Basile, tries to express his somber and
heroic qualities: "Les deux couleurs qu'il évoquait pour elle étaient
le noir et l'or" ("The two colors he evoked for her were black and
gold," 203). It is a complicated and ironic image: intended to convey
an emotional portrait, it also makes concrete links with Le Rouge et
le noir; at the same time, it refers back to a recent description of
the black and gold colors of the imperial flag flying over the fortress,
thus signifying imprisonment and the imperial power to which

Basile aspires but which will finally crush him. Yet, in spite of this concentrated writing, it is questionable whether the best interests of the novel are served by basing it upon a factual event. In *Grimbosq* Peter the Great becomes a tragic, literary character, and the historical material is used as a theme of fatality and as an exotic backdrop. In *Le Prisonnier No. 1.*, however, there is a conflict between the fictional demands of the novel, centered on Basile's obsession and Aglaé's love, and the purely documentary interest of the historical event itself. This conflict, which reappears in the *romans-fleuves*, can sometimes have the effect of limiting the impact of the work by restricting the reader's range of interest. In spite of this potential problem, however, *Le Prisonnier No. 1*, like *Grimbosq*, compares favorably with the preceeding novels to the extent that Troyat is able to escape from the world of Parisian tensions to a landscape in which grandeur and significance are natural.

Viou

Troyat's novel of 1980, *Viou*, marks an end to the Russian excursion in the short fiction but by no means constitutes a return to the contemporary Paris of *Anne Prédaille*. Instead, he profits from a certain "mode rétro" by setting his novel in the provinces just after the end of World War II. Specifically, Troyat has chosen the town of Le Puy, in the Massif Central, where "on ne pouvait marcher dans la rue sans penser à Dieu et aux morts"[16] ("You could not walk in the streets without thinking of God or the dead"). In this setting lives Viou, the six-year-old Sylvie Lesoyeux, whose father Bernard, a doctor in the Haute Savoie, was killed by the Germans in 1944 and whose mother now works in Paris. Viou is being brought up by her grandparents, Hippolyte and Clarisse Lesoyeux, and is only rarely visited by her mother. The simple narrative concentrates on the mind of the young girl as she is faced with the grandmother's cult of the dead Bernard, with the death of her grandfather, the removal of a much-loved pet dog, and the prospect of her mother's remarriage. The novel ends with her leaving Le Puy and taking the train for Paris, where she is met by her new father, Xavier Borderaz.

The novel is the most austere narrative produced by Troyat, and does not really possess a plot at all. Rather, it is constructed on a series of episodes which show the gradual development of Viou herself. Yet, in spite of its austerity, the novel is a successful work in that it just succeeds in avoiding sentimentality and concentrates upon those features in which Troyat excels. In *Viou* he continues his portrait of the young girl, begun with the depiction of Elizabeth Mazalaigue in *La Grive (Elizabeth. A Novel)*. He explores the child's attitude to death: the death of the father, the death of the grandfather, the shocking reality conveyed by the picture of a skeleton. At the same time, he notes Viou's gradual perception of the falsifying power of death: the body of Hippolyte is "grand-père devenu statue" ("grandfather turned into a statue," 164), and the way in which society's own rituals have the same ossifying effect. With the death of the grandfather, his photograph goes to join that of Bernard on the mantle shelf, and Viou reflects: "Pourquoi fallait-il que, l'un après l'autre, les êtres qu'elle aimait se transformaient en photographies?" ("Why was it that, one after the other, the people she loved were transformed into photographs?" 166). This iconography of the dead poses the question of memory, and introduces a favorite subject of Troyat's, the gap between the image and the reality. Throughout all her time in the grandparents' house, Viou cannot connect the ever-present photographs of her father with her own memories of him. Still less can she accept the enormous "portrait grandeur nature" painted by a family friend, M. Poirier, and taken from one of the photographs. It is only by chance that she realizes what is wrong: most of the time her father wore spectacles, but, being vain, took them off to be photographed, hence the deformed, unrecognizable image now left to posterity. Happily, Viou is now able to make the photograph coincide with her memory by the simple expedient of drawing spectacles on the print, but is nevertheless punished by her grandmother, still determined to preserve intact the cult of the dead hero.

As the novel progresses, Troyat is able to show the healthy, positive responses of the young girl. Instinctively she rejects the cult of death: after one of the family's weekly visits to the cemetery, "Sylvie s'aperçut qu'elle s'intéressait plus aux vivants qu'aux morts" ("Sylvie realized that she was more interested in the living than the dead," 136). Similarly, through experience, she is able to accept the selfishness and wrongness of her own reactions. The first occasion concerns her dog Toby, with whom Troyat comes closest to an Orphan-Ann-ish sentimentality. With the death of Hippolyte, the dog pines and Clarisse decides to give him away. At first, Viou is heartbroken, but when, much later, she meets Toby and his new owner, she is forced to recognize his healthiness and the rightness of the grandmother's decision. This episode prepares the reader for the more important acceptance by Viou of her mother's remarriage. At first, she opposes it, using every devious means to fight against it, but is finally persuaded by her mother to leave Le Puy and comes to accept her new father. In this situation, the young child shows a flexibility and maturity denied Gérard Fonsèque or Etienne Martin.

Much of the success of the novel lies in the background against which Viou is portrayed. The novel provides an excellent picture of the day-to-day life of provincial austerity after the war, and depends for its effect, more precisely, on the evocation of the grandparents' house where Viou is brought up. On one level, Troyat appears to be exploiting ground covered by English writers, such as Saki, in "Sredni Vashtar," or Kipling, in "Black Sheep," in his description of a young child being persecuted by a female relative. Thus, Viou is subjected to her grandmother's worship of the dead Bernard and to her strict discipline which becomes almost sadistic. Viou's ally in the household is the more carefree Hippolyte, who has hardly spoken to his wife for years, and who warns her on one occasion: "Je vous conseille de mêler un peu de sucre à votre vinaigre, si vous ne voulez pas nous empoisonner tous" ("I advise you to mix some sugar with your vinegar if you don't want to poison us all," 90). Yet the Lesoyeux family is much more complex than this apparently familiar theme of a group dominated by a death-oriented figure. The grandmother suffers at the indifference of her husband, and to this extent she is as much a victim as a tyrant. Nor is her attitude to Viou one of straightforward censorship: in one curious scene, she invites Viou to her room and there, lovingly, shows the child all the jewels and silver which she will inherit. Finally, at the end of the novel, as Viou leaves the house for Paris, the bond of real affection between grandmother and grandchild becomes apparent.

Nevertheless, in spite of the complicated life of the household, it remains dark and oppressive and in total contrast to the life of Viou's mother: "L'existence de maman paraissait à Sylvie pleine d'imprévu et de légereté" ("her mother's existence seemed to Sylvie to be full of lightness and the unexpected," 103). Significantly, the mother, the grandmother's distrusted daughter-in-law, plays the same role of magician to Viou as does Guillaume to Jean in *Faux Jour*. Her first appearance in the novel coincides with Christmas, when she helps Viou to decorate the tree, and throughout she rep-

resents an accessible and responsible dreamworld removed from the
gloom of the Lesoyeux house. Viou's response to fantasy is intimately
connected with her fascination with language. Troyat notes her love
for her surname, Lesoyeux, because of its sound and its connotations
of smoothness. Similarly, she is aware of language as the constitution
of a reality: one of her favorite sights is the signboard over the
grandfather's coal business, which seems to enshrine the permanence, not merely of their name, but of their existence as well. For
this reason, the change of the sign after Hippolyte's death to "Vil-
leneuve et fils" is more shocking than the grandfather's funeral itself.
Finally, the names establish intimacy between the characters themselves. Troyat emphasizes that the name "Viou" is the result of the
deformation of her Christian name Sylvie to "Sylviou" by her parents. Thus, by the manipulation of names, he is able later to show
the child being won over by her mother's fiancé. On her arrival at
the Paris terminus she is met by Xavier Borderaz, who has brought
his dog with him, which charms Viou in spite of herself and replaces
the absent Toby. At the same time, Borderaz's use of Viou's nickname and his own Christian name cements in a very compressed
manner a father-daughter relationship which is nevertheless a new
friendship.

The success of *Viou* owes much to the fact that it is a novel in
which Troyat takes care not to overreach himself, combining situations which he has described before to convey a modest but effective
faith in happiness and life. At the same time, the unadventurous
nature of the novel constitutes a problem and renders it vulnerable
to charges of seeking easy commercial success through the depiction
of a child in the historically interesting period of the years following
the Liberation. *Viou* is not, therefore, a complete resolution of the
problems which beset the whole of Troyat's short fiction in the
postwar period. On one level, these novels continue to exploit
the themes and preoccupations of the works of the 1930s: psychological weakness and strength, attempts at domination, dream, and
reality. Nor do the later novels move much closer to a solution:
Anne Prédaille continues to dominate, André remains in his dreamworld, Grimbosq and Basile are victims of obsession. Only the child
Viou seems capable of accepting reality without controlling it and
she is, after all, only a child. In order to permutate this restricted
number of themes, Troyat changes the setting of his novels, though
often only to the extent of changing the profession of the protagonist,

and attempts, as in *Une Extrême amitié,* to innovate technically are not wholly successful. For Troyat, the short novel form, like that of Simenon's later psychological novels, permits only a limited number of subjects with limited variations in the narration. It is highly significant that those limitations are only transcended in *Grimbosq* and *Le Prisonnier No. 1,* where Troyat substitutes the material of the *romans-fleuves* for that of the short novels. It remains to be seen whether the technical possibilities offered by the extended novel cycle enable Troyat to discover a more positive escape from the psychological dramas which overwhelm his characters.

Chapter Four
Novel Cycles

Tant que la terre durera

Most critical attention has been focused on Troyat's six novel cycles, *Tant que la terre durera* (1947–50), *Les Semailles et les moissons* (1953–58), *La Lumière des justes* (1959–63), *Les Eygletière* (1965–67), *Les Héritiers de l'avenir* (1968–70), and *Le Moscovite* (1974–76). Together they pose crucial questions about Troyat's literary status: his debt to the continuing French tradition of the *roman-fleuve*, from Balzac and Zola, through Romain Rolland to the novelists of the 1930s, Martin du Gard, Duhamel, and Romains; his use of the German *Bildungsroman* and the family novel; his exploitation of nineteenth-century Russian fiction. At the same time, there is an intrusion of more popular commercial elements, owing much to the tradition of the *feuilleton* and postwar exotic historical novels such as *Gone with the Wind* and *Forever Amber*. The intermingling of these elements shows also the role of the traditional status of the *roman-fleuve* as a means to combating a changing world.

Tant que la terre durera constitutes a new departure in Troyat's fiction and is only permitted by the change in scope and writing involved in the 1940 biography of Dostoevski. This apprenticeship in conveying the entire career of an individual, with the relevant social and political context, enables Troyat to move away from the short psychological novels toward the broader canvas of the *roman-fleuve*. His first novel cycle, written during the Occupation and the postwar period, took ten years to write and, as three 800-page volumes in the *Table Ronde* edition, it is the longest of his extended fictional works. It is also the broadest in historical terms, moving from the *Belle Epoque* of the "temps du dernier tsar" ("age of the last czar"), through the Russo-Japanese War, the 1905 Revolution, World War I, the two revolutions of 1917, and ending with the outbreak of World War II in 1939.

The first volume, *Tant que la terre durera* (1947), establishes the novel as a family novel, concentrating upon the family of Constantin Kirollovitch Arapoff, a doctor in Ekaterinoder. Into this family comes Michel Danoff, the son of a rich Circassian draper of Armavir, who marries the doctor's eldest daughter Tania. Henceforth the novel, throughout its three volumes, is centered upon the fortunes of Michel and Tania and their children, but follows also the careers of the other members of the Arapoff family: the quiet profound Nina, who becomes a nurse; Lioubov, the actress; Akim, the career army officer; and Nicolas who moves toward the Bolsheviks. As the first volume progresses, it shows the Danoff business prospering in the last years of the czar's reign, with Michel and Tania establishing themselves in luxury in Moscow. At the same time, signs of catastrophe, both personal and political, become visible. Akim, after a successful career at officer school, is posted to his beloved Hussards d'Alexandria, only to make the long journey to Manchuria and witness the humiliating defeat of the Russian army at the hands of the Japanese.

Nicholas, irreversibly politicized by witnessing the massacre of the protesters of 1905 led by the priest Gapone, is in a privileged position to spot the crumbling of the empire's foundations. In private terms, the family is shocked by the activities of Lioubov, who not only thrives in the unrespectable context of the theater but contracts a disastrous and short-lived marriage with the sinister Kisiakoff and takes a lover, the fellow-actor Prychkine. Nor are the Danoffs themselves immune from disaster. Michel neglects Tania for his business, and she falls in love instead with his best friend, Volodia, who is spurred on by Kisiakoff who adopts him as his son. The volume ends in 1914, with Tania's confession of infidelity and Michel's decision to leave for the war.

Le Sac et la cendre (Sackcloth and Ashes, 1948) continues the story from 1914 to 1920, but concentrates on the Revolution and the Civil War. The novel shows the growing strength of the revolutionary movement through the activities of Nicolas and the disintegration of the army by the experiences of the regiment of hussars in which Akim and Michel serve. After the capture of the Winter Palace in St. Petersburg by the Bolsheviks in October 1917, the liberal provisional government of Kerensky falls, to be replaced by the Soviet regime. From this point onward, the lives of the rich Moscow merchants change radically, and when Michel, long given up for dead, returns to Tania, he discovers a house which has been almost totally requisitioned and an atmosphere of threat hanging over his family. Definitively reconciled, Michel and Tania plan their flight from Moscow, under the discreet protection of the now powerful Nicolas. Michel leaves first for the south, followed by Tania, the Swiss governess, and the two sons, Boris and Serge. After an epic journey, beset by corrupt officials, partisans, and disease, the family is reunited in the Caucassus, while awaiting the victory of Korniloff's czarist loyalists over the Bolsheviks. Yet, as Akim discovers at the head of his regiment, the men are no longer immune to revolutionary propaganda, and the loyalist cause is lost. The volume ends with the Danoff family leaving on the boat for exile in Europe. Behind them, they leave Volodia, denounced by Kisiakoff and executed by the revolutionaries, Nicolas, shot by White Russian partisans during the Civil War, Lioubov, who now plays with as much fervor and as much success to the Bolsheviks as she did to the czar, and the father of the family, Dr. Arapoff, who finally succumbs to a heart attack. The past is now definitively dead.

The attempt to come to terms with that fact, through the experience of exile, is the theme of the final volume of the series, *Etrangers sur la terre (Strangers in the Land,* 1950). Michel and Tania are now established in Paris but find it increasingly difficult to survive financially. This collapse of their fortune culminates in their furniture being seized by the bailiffs and their enforced removal to a smaller apartment. At the same time, they are unable to adjust to a situation in which their temporary exile has become, to any objective observer, permanent. This inadaptability is rendered more poignant by the development of their two sons: Boris rejects the Russian émigré community, with its pathetic illusory faith in an imminent collapse of the Soviet regime, and feels himself French to the extent of assuming French nationality and marrying a French girl, Odile; Serge, however, falls under the still malignant influence of Kisiakoff, who involves him in a squalid affair with an aging rich woman, Lucienne Pérez. Kisiakoff's power for evil is not definitive, however, and, with the suicide of his mistress, Serge is able to break away. Shortly after, Kisiakoff dies in his turn. Nor is Boris's decision to be naturalized French negative in its effect on his parents. It induces Michel to take a realistic view of the long-term nature of their residence in France and impels him to abandon the increasingly chimerical money-making schemes which link him with the father in *Faux Jour* in favor of a return to the origins of his career: he opens a small draper's shop, the original Comptoirs Danoff, begun by his father a generation ago. In this enterprise, Michel and Tania show positive qualities absent in Akim and Nina, who have similarly fled to Paris. Akim, with Nina as his housekeeper, has retreated into the past by turning his apartment into a regimental museum for the Hussards d'Alexandria. That this service to the memory of the past is unreal and no proof against the present is confirmed by Akim's absurd accidental death on the peripheries of the rioting of 6 February 1934. It is the positive middle way represented by Michel and Tania and Boris which is capable of resisting the evil influence of Kisiakoff, the irresponsibility of Lioubov and Serge, and the unreality of Akim. It is a choice rewarded by continuity and survival: as Boris leaves for his unit in September 1939, Michel and Tania visit his wife Odile and their newborn grandson: "Ecoute, Tania. . . . Tu entends? . . . C'est lui . . . Michel . . . Michel Borissovitch Danoff"[1] ("Listen Tania. . . . Can you hear? . . . It's him. . . . Michel. . . . Michel Borrissovitch Danoff").

Tant que la terre durera constitutes the chronological final phase in Troyat's treatment of Russian history in his novels. The subsequent cycles—*La Lumière des justes, Les Héritiers de l'avenir,* and *Le Moscovite*—go back into the nineteenth century to find the deeper causes of the collapse of the empire recounted in the first *roman-fleuve.* Nevertheless, all four novels, whatever their individual literary merits, possess a broad thematic unity, concentrating upon the issue of Franco-Russian relations, the ambiguity of exile, the role of the individual in the context of major historical events. This last theme informs the whole of *Tant que la terre durera:* in spite of their relative wealth, the Danoffs are not powerful enough to exert political influence. Instead, they are the privileged victims of a disaster they can do nothing to prevent: even Nicolas is a peripheral figure in the Bolshevik organization and he dies a solitary death, where what power he has is useless. It is in the last volume of the cycle that Troyat expresses for the first time the problems of the relationship between France and Russia and the broader question of exile. In *Etrangers sur la terre,* the Danoffs' Russian culture comes into conflict for the first time with an alien one, that of their adoptive homeland. Through this encounter, Troyat is able to outline the basic differences between the two civilizations and also to chart the difficulties of assimilation. This becomes largely a question of generations: Michel's mother, Maria Ossipovna, resolutely believes herself to be in Moscow and spends her exile battling with the topography of Paris. Michel and Tania occupy a median position between the deluded grandmother and the younger gen~ation, but, because of mainly linguistic barriers, cling to their Russian origins and refuse the attractions of French culture. It is the younger Russian exiles, represented by Boris, who are able to manipulate the French language and accept the culture and who come to regard the life-style of their parents as alien and illusory. At the same time, Boris's French naturalization does not turn him into a complete Frenchman: he remains in that fascinating situation of irony for Troyat, the product of two cultures and two languages, and no longer totally at home in either. This ambiguity looks forward to the anomalous position of Sophie in *La Lumière des justes,* and of Armand de Croué in *Le Moscovite.* It also introduces the more general and poignant theme of exile, which receives its fullest treatment in the final volume of *Les Héritiers de l'avenir.* What Troyat analyzes with affection and pity are the most characteristic traits of exile psychology: the conviction that exile is only temporary and that reinstatement is inevitable, and the re-creation of the original life-style, through an intense communal activity and retention of pre-exile customs, language, food, and religion. That these traits should be so vulnerable to the passage of time is the major source of the tragedy of exile.

In order to establish this vast historical picture of the rise and fall of the Russian commercial bourgeoisie, Troyat adopts two major techniques of realist fiction: documentation and apparent impartiality. He recounts, in *Un si long chemin,* that the novel was based on extensive reminiscences of his parents, both concerning their adventures in the flight from Moscow and, perhaps more important, their daily life in affluent Russia. Similarly, the topographical detail in the first two volumes was established and confirmed by Troyat's use of a 1900 Baedecker guide to Moscow, a technique which the author has consistently used ever since.[2] This careful documentation, combined with detailed historical knowledge of the period 1880–1920, establishes the realistic foundations of that autonomous fictional world essential to the relationship between the reader and the *roman-fleuve* itself. One result of the historical credibility of the novel is the unusually extreme impartiality of the narrator. The characters are followed with comprehension and sympathy, even when they adopt diametrically opposed positions. Thus, Troyat is able to depict the revolutionary, Nicolas, and the reactionary officer, Akim, in an equally favorable light. It is merely sufficient for the novel's perspective to change for the political position to change with it. This aspect of the novel, apparently of only technical importance, has considerable general implications. In the first place, it asserts the primacy of character in the *roman-fleuve* and the subordination of abstract considerations, be they ethical or political, to the privileged relationship between the narrator and the cast. Second, it places the emphasis of the novel upon features which are common to all the characters and which do not separate them on merely ideological lines. In this case, the common denominator is the Hegelian omnipotence of history and the consequent weakness of human happiness, though this is shown to be the product, not merely of irresistible political forces, but also of human inconstancy and instability. In this way, Troyat uses the possibilities of the genre to introduce a very general theme indeed, a view of human development in terms of cyclical repetition within each generation. As he comments in *Un si long chemin:* "Quant au personnage principal du livre, pour moi, c'est le temps. Ce que j'ai voulu exprimer, c'est le recommencement des amours, des angoisses, des passions politiques, des joies familiales, des deuils, des ambitions, d'une génération à l'autre. Chacun croit être le premier à vivre une expérience, et il est le millième interprète d'un rôle vieux comme le monde" ("The principal character in the book for me is time. I wanted to express the repetition of love affairs, anxieties, political passions, family joys, mourning, ambitions, from one generation to another. Everyone thinks that they are the first to have an experience, when they are the thousandth interpreter of a part which is as old as the world," 100).

Within the context of the frailty of the individual against historical forces and the unending repetition of human action and emotion, however, Troyat nevertheless permits a distinction between positive and inauthentic responses. His sympathy is with the Chekhovian Doctor Arapoff, the gentle, practical, and humane doctor, and with Michel and Tania who, in their long journey through infidelity and violence and exile, come to a serene and positive acceptance of their fallen state. Troyat admires strength, practicality, and authenticity. For this reason his weak characters, like Volodia

or Serge, are punished, as those who retreat into hypocrisy like
Lioubov, a hypocrisy once more signified by Troyat's favorite theater
image, or an unreal world, like Akim in his tragic last days, are
implicitly condemned. In the face of wide-scale historical disaster,
Troyat is able to anchor his fiction in a modest humanity.

Yet it is a humanity threatened by more than the Bolsheviks. In
Kisiakoff, Troyat has created one of his most extraordinary characters
and one whom, understandably, he was reluctant to kill off, even
at a late stage in the third volume.[3] From his entry into the Arapoff
family as Lioubov's husband, to his corruption of Serge Danoff in
Etrangers sur la terre, Kisiakoff is permanently present as a source of
metaphysical evil. Troyat refers to him in *Un si long chemin* as a
"Raspoutine rigolard" ("a jolly Rasputin," 103), but his real role
is that of the Devil figure who inhabits the short stories and novellas.
His invocation of God at the inception of each evil action places
him in a Luciferian position; more specifically, his task is to feed
upon the weaknesses of the other characters: Lioubov's theatricality,
the naivete of Nicolas and the 1905 revolutionaries, the sensuality
of Volodia, the adolescent rebelliousness of Serge. In this sense, he
is the Devil of the czar's bourgeoisie and he presides over their
emotional bankruptcy and political downfall. Significantly, his death
coincides with the recuperation of Serge and the Danoffs' healthy
acceptance of their new setting and status. The ambition and inauthenticity upon which this vibrant and sinister figure has fed are
finally transmuted into positive emotion, and he can only disappear.
Nevertheless, the gradually achieved dominant role which he occupies in the novel indicates a degree of pessimism in Troyat's
contemplation of humanity based, not on historical vulnerability,
but upon the persistence in the human psyche of ineradicable flaws
which constitute the only evil of the age. It is for this reason that,
in the fantastic atmosphere of the *contes,* the Devil himself appears,
and, in the subsequent *romans-fleuves,* the will to historical change
is wrecked repeatedly upon unalterable human failings.

Les Semailles et les moissons

The strength of *Tant que la terre durera* lies in its skillful depiction
of an extended bourgeois family in the grip of complex and dramatic
historical events. In the five volumes of *Les Semailles et les moissons,*
Troyat chooses to write the French counterpart of his first *roman-*

fleuve, describing the ascension of a provincial petit-bourgeois family and its evolution under the Third Republic, World War I, and the Occupation. The selection of the title, which is the second component in the biblical quotation, "Tant que la terre durera, les semailles et les moissons, le froid et le chaud, l'été et l'hiver, le jour et la nuit ne cesseront point de s'entre-suivre"[4] ("While the earth remaineth, seedtime and harvest, and cold and heat, and summer and winter, and day and night shall not cease"), indicates its close relationship to the preceding novel and announces the way in which the two plots interlink at the end of the fifth volume. To this extent, *Tant que la terre durera* and *Les Semailles et les moissons* must be read together as one single Franco-Russian novel.

The first volume, *Les Semailles et les moissons* (1953), begins in a small village in the Corrèze before World War I and describes the Aubernat family: Jérôme, the local blacksmith, his wife Maria who runs the village's general store, and their two children, Amélie, who in spite of her *Brevet d'études* and her ambition to teach, helps her mother, and her younger brother Denis. The family's way of life is shattered by the death of Maria from tuberculosis, and it is the capable Amélie who replaces her as head of the household, caring for the grief-stricken Jérôme and the unruly Denis. She is about to be imprisoned by her own family and by her forthcoming marriage to the worthy but boring Jean Eyrolles when she is swept off her feet by Pierre Mazalaigue, the son of the local café proprietor. They are quickly married and Pierre and Amélie move to Paris where Pierre has found work. His job, however, involves long periods of absence, and he finally gives it up in favor of taking up a dilapidated bar in Montmartre. Here, the practicality and hard work of Pierre and Amélie come into their own and they manage to build up a popular and prosperous business. The idyll is destroyed, however, by the declaration of World War I, and Pierre is conscripted while Amélie is forced to close the bar and return to the Corrèze to await the birth of their daughter, Elizabeth. The second volume, *Amélie* (1955), sees the heroine back in charge of the café in the rue de Montreuil and develops her qualities of organization and self-sufficiency. Much of the novel concentrates on her day-to-day management of the bar while caring for the baby and her brother Denis who has come to help her. The one single episode which shows these positive qualities, however, describes her frustration at being separated from Pierre and her determination to visit him behind the lines at Toul. Tenaciously, she manages to overcome all the obstacles placed in her way and is able to meet her husband, only to discover the tragic effects of the demoralization of the trenches. Her return to Paris is followed by Pierre being reported missing and by her subsequent discovery that he is in hospital in Orléans with a serious head wound. The novel ends with Amélie's decision to take Pierre to convalesce in the Corrèze, but not before she has signed the contract to purchase a larger café, the *Cristal,* in the rue de Rochechouart.

La Grive (1956) begins to move the reader's interest away from the older generation of Pierre, Amélie, and Denis to the development of the daughter, Elizabeth. The first part of the novel describes the eight-year-old child's fascination with the world of the Montmartre café, still largely run by Amélie and Denis, since Pierre has not fully recovered from his head wound which has rendered him impotent and liable to fits of irrational temper. Elizabeth is sickly, however, and is advised to leave Paris for the country. She is enrolled in a *pensionnat* in the Lot, run by Mademoiselle Quercy. Throughout this long episode, Troyat deals sensitively with the evolution of a young girl, her loneliness, her coquettishness, her period of intense religiosity, and her violent rebellion provoked by the death of a friend. Mlle Quercy finally recognizes Elizabeth's inadaptability to the life of the school, and she is sent instead to her aunt and uncle at La Jeyzelou, in the Corrèze, where the novel ends with her being brought up in an atmosphere of kindness and freedom. In the subsequent volume, *Tendre et violente Elizabeth* (1957), Elizabeth is now nineteen and her parents have moved from Paris to a hotel in the ski resort of Megève in the French Alps. The novel depicts the life of the resort through the hotel, but concentrates on Elizabeth's first love affair with the cynical German teacher Christian Walter. In a moment of rage at being deceived by Christian, she accepts the offer of marriage of one of the hotel guests, the weak composer Patrice Monastier. The final episodes show her inability to adapt to the secluded existence of the Monastier family home in Saint Germain-en-Laye and the continued attraction exerted by Christian, who visits Paris frequently. She finally discovers that she is expecting Christian's child and, in despair, is persuaded to leave her husband and go to Switzerland for an abortion. The volume ends with her desperate appeal for help to her mother. The last volume in the series, *La Rencontre* (1958), runs from the Munich crisis of 1938 to the

Liberation and begins with Elizabeth firmly established as the owner of a record shop near the Champs Elysées. In a serious attempt to assert her independence, she abandons Christian, but immediately falls under the influence of the much weaker Bertrand Lesaulnier, a married businessman. Their love affair is destroyed by the fall of France in 1940 and Elizabeth is reunited with her parents and grandfather in the Corrèze. With the signing of the Armistice, she decides to return to Paris and goes to Tulle to get the necessary papers. There she meets Patrice who, like Charles Madrier, is in the *Intendance,* and he introduces her to a friend, Boris Danoff, whose wife and child have been killed during the German invasion. The last part of the novel is set in Paris during the Occupation and brings Boris and Elizabeth close together, despite the pain that this causes Patrice, who goes off to die in the Resistance. Boris survives his own Resistance involvement and he and Elizabeth are married, thus joining the Danoff and Mazalaigue families and the two novel cycles. The novel ends with Boris and Elizabeth standing on the roof of their apartment, listening to the bells of Notre Dame announcing the Liberation of Paris.

Les Semailles et les moissons has been criticized in literary manuals for failing to come up to the standards of the previous *roman-fleuve.* This criticism is based largely upon the premise that Troyat, not being French, is writing about an area which he knows imperfectly and that therefore the novel lacks the realist authenticity of *Tant que la terre durera*. This criticism is as unfortunate as it is erroneous. In *Un si long chemin* he describes how the novel is documented from experiences from the childhood of his second wife Guite,[5] who was brought up in the Corrèze, and establishes the novel's realist credentials. In fact, prerevolutionary Russia is as far removed from Troyat's own experience as pre–World War I France, and he has used the same techniques to evoke both periods: historical research, and the gathering of eyewitness information. What such criticism obscures are the very real literary qualities of the work. The evocation of the cafés in the first three volumes and the depiction of a struggling petite bourgeoisie show Troyat's award of the Prix Populiste for *Faux Jour* to be amply, if retrospectively, justified. There are few better populist novels in France than *Amélie,* which avoids the romanticization of Montmartre of the novels of Carco and the fragmentation of Dabit's *Hôtel du Nord* (1929). The novel, with its surrounding scenes in the preceding and subsequent volumes, is a

moving and authentic picture of the life of the *petites gens* before the
war and the effect of the holocaust upon their modest existence: it
is Troyat writing at his very best and it merits inclusion in any
serious consideration of the twentieth-century French novel. Similarly, the analysis of the child Elizabeth in *La Grive* is a sensitive
attempt to come to terms with the world of the very young, with
its exaggerated anxieties, its vulnerability, and its rapid and easy
reassurance. Even more than *Viou*, the novel manages to remain on
the realist side of sentimentality and constitutes one of the few
successful novels of childhood.

It is all the more disappointing, therefore, given the high promise
of the first three volumes, that *Tendre et violente Elizabeth* should be
such a failure. By moving the action from the mid-1920s to the
mid-1930s and by following the Mazalaigue's upward social mobility from café owners to hoteliers, Troyat enters areas which he
is unable to depict convincingly. Whereas his description of the rue
de Rochechouart has a weight and a density which renders it credible, his evocation of the hotel in the two-dimensional world of the
ski resort, apart from isolated episodes such as the arrival of the
Russian chef, remains conventional and plays upon the stock responses of his readers. It is a geographical and social shift which
takes him dangerously close to the world of the commercial popular
novel, in which the rich at leisure have always been an attractive
subject. Similarly, if *La Grive* is a careful and penetrating study of
childhood, his depiction of Elizabeth as a young woman is discon-
certingly superficial.

It is interesting that, in most of his short novels, Troyat should
avoid descriptions of love affairs: it is not an area in which he excels
and it is a subject which rarely coincides with his real preoccupations.
Such are the demands of the *roman-fleuve*, however, that it is an area
which it is difficult to omit; yet it is never successfully dealt with.
To denote passion, Troyat relies upon the *coup de foudre*, as psychologically unexplained as it is intrusive. Elizabeth becomes the model
for his subsequent heroines by being willful and resourceful, yet
curiously passive and powerless toward any character who cries "Je
t'aime!" Her decision to definitively reject Christian Walter is admirable and consistent with her character; her immediate psychological self-abasement before Bertrand Lesaulnier is merely
improbable. This defect is connected with Troyat's inability to create
convincing male lovers who, while totally authentic in their profes-

sional lives, become melodramatically dominating in their sexual relationships. Pierre Mazalaigue's insistent courtship of Amélie is a case in point, and his psychological authenticity is only reestablished with the dominance of the professional life in the café and the eradication of his sexuality after the war.

More damaging for the novel is Elizabeth's first lover, Christian Walter, who comes in the middle of a long line of charismatic predators, from Kisiakoff to Alexandre Kozlov, in *Les Eygletière*. The problem is that Christian lacks the extraordinary dimensions of Kisiakoff and his credentials as an exceptional being are only established by a repetitious cynicism and a simplistic amoralism. In other words, Christian is the stereotype of the mysterious intelligent stranger in the ski resort, a character of popular fiction who has no place in the serious realist novel that *Les Semailles et les moissons* aspires to be.[6] It is an indication of *Tendre et violente Elizabeth*'s failure that even the succeeding novel, with its powerful theme of the Occupation and the Liberation, is unable to totally retrieve it.

Despite the defects of the last two volumes, among which must be added Troyat's inability to retain contact with all his characters (Christian vanishes in the first part of the last volume; Denis is consigned to a German prisoner of war camp and forgotten), the cycle as a whole raises some important issues. A feature of Troyat's *romans-fleuves* emerges here which will be repeated in subsequent cycles: an interest in his female characters as the repository of realism, practicality, and strength, while the men are often deluded or weak. It is Amélie who is the source of the family's upward mobility, and Elizabeth's easy domination of the pathetic Patrice and the weak Bertrand is characteristic of Troyat's extended fiction as a whole. This, in its turn, introduces a further preoccupation: the role of hereditary characteristics transmitted through the female members of the family.

Maria, Amélie, and Elizabeth all possess the same independence of spirit which allows them to govern their partners. At the same time, they have in common certain less admirable traits, particularly the ability to overreact irrationally to any supposed slight. Yet this emotional continuity reaffirms the novel's main lesson: the constant elements of humanity in the midst of violent historical change. It is this which constitutes the meaning of the title: the first volume begins with the death of the mother and ends with the birth of Elizabeth; the whole cycle goes through war and death and emotional turmoil to conclude with a marriage and the bells of liberation. This apparently optimistic theme is reinforced by Jérôme's mystical fascination with the remains of the old Roman settlement at Veixou, above his village: it guarantees survival and the continuity of man. Yet this example is not without disquieting qualities: at the end of *L'Espoir*, as the Republican forces drive to victory at Guadalajara, Malraux chooses to depict the guide of the old ruined city, who comments on the permanence of stones and the frailty of human projects.[7] In the same way, Troyat's emphasis in his first two novel cycles on the eternal, repetitive, and unchanging quality of human existence can be read either as an affirmation of the irreducible characteristics of humanity or as the expression of a deep-rooted and disquieting fatalism by which human action is of minimal importance and where the Russian Revolution, the Great War, and the Liberation pale into insignificance in the light of the great cosmic movement of history.

La Lumière des justes

In his next *roman-fleuve* Troyat moves away from twentieth-century France and back to Russia in the nineteenth century, a period which he has already closely documented in the biographies of Dostoevski and Pushkin and his 1956 essay, *La Vie quotidienne en Russie au temps du dernier tsar (Daily Life in Russia under the Last Czar)*. The first volume, (*Les Compagnons du coquelicot (The Brotherhood of the Red Poppy*, 1959), is set mainly in Paris during the Allied occupation of 1814–15, and shows the effect of French Republican philosophies upon the young czarist officers who had left their country for the first time as a result of the Napoleonic Wars, and who were to instigate the Decembrist uprising against Nicholas I in 1825.

Nicolas Ozéroff (Ozareff in later volumes) is a lieutenant in the *Gardes de Lithuanie* and is fascinated by the life of the French capital during the restoration of Louis XVIII and Napoleon's 100 Days. He falls in love with the daughter of the French family with whom he is billetted, the widowed Sophie de Lambrefous, and is introduced by her into a Republican group, the "Compagnons du coquelicot." In spite of his father's initial opposition to the concept of a French Catholic daughter-in-law, Nicolas marries Sophie and takes her to Russia in the deluded belief that the *fait accompli* of their wedding will set things right. Sophie therefore enters the Ozéroff house in

Kachtanovka, near Pskov, only to have her illusions shattered by the brutal reception of Nicolas's father, Michel Borissovitch. The novel ends with their flight from the family estate to St. Petersburg. *La Barynia* (*The Baroness*, 1960) begins with the birth of Sophie's son and her reconciliation with Nicolas's father. Her child dies, and the couple return to Kachtanovka where Sophie befriends her sister-in-law, Marie, and exerts increasing influence upon the household. Her idyllic life as *barynia* ("lady of the manor") is destroyed, however, by two events: Marie falls under the influence of a sinister neighbor, Vladimir Karpovitch Sédoff and marries him in spite of his brutality and infidelity; Nicolas, bored in the provinces, has a tawdry affair with the mother of a friend, Vassia Valkoff, the discovery of which breaks the innocence of the marriage. The novel ends with Marie, abandoned by Sédoff, giving birth to a son and committing suicide, and with Nicolas returning to St. Petersburg and being involved in the conspiracy which resulted in the Decembrist uprising.

La Gloire des vaincus (The glory of the vanquished, 1961) opens on the eve of the Decembrist coup, in the confusion over the succession to Alexander I. Here, in considerable detail, Troyat shows the preparations for the revolt, with the weakness and illusions of the participants, and the *débâcle* of 14 December 1925, consolidating the position of Czar Nicolas I. In spite of Nicolas's prominent position in the organization of the uprising, he is not immediately arrested and sets out for Kachtanovka with his servant Nikita in order to see Sophie and win her back. He is arrested on the way, however, and imprisoned in the Peter and Paul fortress. There, in spite of her father-in-law's calumnies, Sophie rejoins her husband and is reconciled with him, and when Nicolas escapes the capital punishment meted out to Rykyev and the other leaders of the rebellion and is sentenced to imprisonment in Siberia, she follows the example of the wives of the other prisoners and attempts to join him. The remainder of the volume describes her efforts to gain authorization from Count Benckendorf, the czar's chief of police, and her arduous journey from St. Petersburg to Siberia with the servant Nikita. She is eventually reunited with Nicolas in Chita, but only after, unbeknown to her, Nikita has been killed by gendarmes.

The fourth volume, *Les Dames de Sibérie* (The ladies of Siberia, 1962), deals with the Decembrists' exile. In the first part Sophie becomes accustomed to life in Chita but, after all her adventures, experiences a sense of anticlimax to the extent that she no longer loves Nicolas. This feeling is accentuated by her grief at the news of Nikita's death and the realization that she loved him. The crisis is resolved, however, when the prisoners are moved from Chita to Pétrovsk: during the journey, Nicolas, in despair at his wife's indifference, endeavors to escape and contracts dysentery. It is in caring for her recaptured husband that Sophie rediscovers her love for him, a love which lasts throughout the novel. The imprisonment in Pétrovsk, in spite of its hardship, is rendered humane by the relative freedom accorded the Decembrists and by the gruff kindness shown by the commandant, the Pole General Léparsky. It is during this period that news reaches Nicolas and Sophie of the death of Michel Borissovitch and his decision to cut his son out of his will and to divide his property between Sophie and Marie's son Serge. An amnesty is finally granted, and Nicolas and Sophie are exiled to the remote fishing hamlet of Mertvy Koultouk on the shores of Lake Baikal, near the Chinese border. It is here that Nicolas dies, killed by a freak storm while fishing on the lake, and Sophie remains alone in exile.

Sophie, ou la fin des combats (Sophie, or the end of the struggle, 1963) moves the novel forward to seventeen years after Nicolas's death. Sophie is now fifty-seven, living in the exile community of Tobolsk. All the old emnities between the exiled wives are now forgotten and Sophie lives a quiet, comfortable existence, gently falling in love with the humane doctor, Ferdinand Wolff. Ironically, her happiness is destroyed by her unexpected liberation and her enforced return to Kachtanovka, now managed by her nephew Serge. The journey from Siberia proves to take her to an even darker imprisonment: Serge has inherited the cynical and unscrupulous characteristics of his father, whom he is widely suspected of having murdered, and consigns his aunt to virtual house arrest. Sophie's position becomes so intolerable that she requests the authorization to return to her native France.

But her homecoming and her establishment in the rue de Grenelle prove to be yet another stage in her continuing exile. Her frequentation of Russian émigrés around the Princess Lieven, and her renewal of acquaintanceship with the revolutionary Vavasseur, render her socially unacceptable and politically suspect at the time of the Crimean War. Sickened by the hypocrisy of her Parisian friends and saddened by the news of the death of Doctor Wolff, Sophie feels utterly isolated when she hears that Serge has been killed by his own serfs. Kachtanovka now belongs entirely to her and is the only place where she can escape her constant exile. The liberal French aristocrat finally finds peace on a Russian feudal estate.

La Lumière des justes analyzes the origins of the revolutionary opposition to czarist autocracy which brings down the regime in 1917. As such, it ends with the death of the unyielding Nicholas I and the liberation of the serfs under the more liberal Alexander II in 1861 which, in its turn, is the point of departure for Troyat's third Russian novel cycle, *Les Héritiers de l'avenir*. Yet Troyat's depiction of revolutionary activity and its impact upon man's historical development is no more optimistic than in *Tant que la terre durera*. His description of the Decembrists emphasizes their political naiveté and impracticality and concentrates upon the incoherence of the whole enterprise. The conspirators are shown to be irremediably aristocratic, motivated less by a desire to see French radical ideology implemented in Russia than by a purely dynastic belief in the claim to the throne of Grand Duke Constantine. Their politicization takes place with their arrest, imprisonment, and exile, rather than in the conspiratorial phase.

At the same time, Troyat is aware that this childlike aristocratic rebellion is the beginning of a process which will pervade Russian society and finally overturn it. At the end of Sophie's exile in Tobolsk, a new consignment of political prisoners arrives, the "Pétrachevsky," a revolutionary group which included Dostoevski, who appears in person in the novel. The members of this group are conscious of their role in a continuing process; as one member says to Sophie: "Après vingt-cinq ans de martyre, vous venez au secours de ceux qui ont pris votre relève!"[8] ("After twenty-five years of suffering, you have come to the aid of those who have taken up your task!). More specifically, the "Pétrachevsky" are important as predominantly bourgeois conspirators: the revolution is descending the social scale, with the implication that once it reaches the proletariat the final explosion will come. Confronted by this irreversible process, Troyat adopts a disabused but nostalgic liberal position, not dissimilar to that adopted by Camus, whose play *Les Justes* may have given rise to the title of the novel, as it did to the subject matter of the radio play *L'Assassinat d'Alexandre II*.

At the very beginning of the Decembrist conspiracy, Troyat indicates a deep distrust of a philosophy which was to become that
of Bolshevism: "La révolution sera l'oeuvre d'une élite. Le peuple
bénéficiera des résultats sans avoir combattu pour les obtenir, sans
même, en fait, les avoir désirés!"[9]—("The revolution will be the
work of an elite. The people will benefit from the results without
fighting to obtain them, without indeed even wanting them!)—a
comment which poses the traditional liberal dilemma, how to abolish an unpalatable social system without espousing the very principles on which that system is based. As Nicolas despairingly asks,
"La grandeur d'un état est-elle incompatible avec le bonheur de ses
sujets?"[10] ("Is the greatness of a nation incompatible with the happiness of its subjects?"), an incompatibility crystallized by the liberal
General Léparsky, the Pole who governs the prison in Pétrovsk and
who (in Les Dames de Sibérie) gloomily recognizes that "il n'y avait
que des prisonniers en Russie, du haut en bas de l'échelle sociale"
("there were only prisoners in Russia, from top to bottom of the
social scale," 222), and that he, because of his own contradictions,
is powerless.

If Russia itself is seen as a vast prison, an image which may reflect
the age of Stalin, it stands also as a metaphor for human existence
itself, beset by varying degrees of evil. Kachtanovka becomes the
center of this: the cruelty meted out to the peasants, the thoughtless
infidelity of Nicolas, the sinister domination of Michel Borissovitch,
an aging "araigne," and, most strikingly, the period in which Victor
Sédoff and his son Serge run the estate with an arbitrary despotism
which mirrors that of the autocracy itself.

Nor is the evil confined to Kachtanovka: it radiates out in petty
but mortal rays—the hostility of the other "dames de Sibérie"
toward Sophie's disaffection with Nicolas, the brusque isolation of
Sophie in Paris—make a mockery of the superficial optimism of
the novel's title, taken from the biblical quotation: "La lumière des
justes donne la joie. La lampe des méchants s'éteindra" ("The light
of the righteous rejoiceth: but the lamp of the wicked shall be put
out").[11] Yet, against this background of evil stands Troyat's heroine.
Nicolas is never meant to achieve the stature of his wife: his understanding is consistently impaired and his character lacks strength.
There is a large element of game-playing in his activities in which
he plays at revolution as he plays at marriage. Yet Sophie trium-
phantly transcends her husband's weakness: through exile in Russia,

torture by Michel Borissovitch, the loss of her child, Nicolas's betrayal, her journey to Siberia, the death of her lover and her husband, she maintains a dignity and attains an authenticity which confer upon her a genuinely tragic status. In the prison of Siberia she achieves an existentialist sense of freedom: "Pour la première fois depuis sa rélégation, elle choisissait la Sibérie. Elle se dit même, avec une pointe d'orgueil, qu'elle la choisissait *librement*" ("For the first time since her exile, she chose Siberia. She even said, with a touch of pride, that she chose it *freely*"). [12]

For, if *La Lumière des justes* is a long prison novel, it is also a novel of exile in which Troyat takes up and amplifies the preoccupations of *Tant que la terre durera*. In comparison with that of Nicolas or the other ladies of Siberia, Sophie's exile is exceedingly complex: physically, she is exiled from Paris to Kachtanovka, from Kachtanovka to Siberia, and, finally with cruel irony, from Siberia to Paris. Culturally, she has entered that limbo which will become familiar to Armand de Croué in *Le Moscovite*, where she is alienated from her own country without being totally accepted by her adoptive one. This ambiguity culminates in her return to France under the Second Empire, when she is unable to sympathize with Napoleon III's ambitions in the Crimea and feels strangely alienated from her compatriots. In its turn, this cultural exile is compounded by an emotional one in which Sophie, for large sections of the novel, is indifferent to Nicolas and where she is separated by her caste and, ultimately, by death from her authentic love for Nikita. Sophie's final return to Kachtanovka is a homecoming in which national, political, and sentimental differences are all resolved and which she so richly deserves.

La Lumière des justes must count among Troyat's fictional successes. The technical mastery with which he organizes the five volumes and manipulates his characters and historical material is considerable. Sophie de Lambrefous becomes one of his most impressive creations; and the thematic areas in which he is able to take the work—unconquerable evil, human weakness, political ineffectualness, exile—confer a weight and a humanity often missing in the shorter novels. Nor, apart from Sophie's winning over of her father-in-law and her love for Nikita, does Troyat risk the use of fictional cliché, though in both cases he finally escapes, by having Nikita die and by transforming Michel Borissovitch into a monster. His denial that it is "de l'histoire romancée" is justified to the extent that he is able to create immediate and convincing characters and raise questions of enduring importance. The inclusion in the novel of material used in the Dostoevski and Pushkin biographies, the use of historical characters, such as Dostoevski himself, Benckendorf, and the original Decembrists, are in danger of reducing the impact of the work from the aesthetic to the historical.

Unlike the previous *romans-fleuves*, *La Lumière des justes* does not open out into the recent past: in spite of its general thematic importance and contemporary political analogies, it remains imprisoned in the nineteenth century, appealing to an antiquarian as well as a fictional interest. Nor can the problem be resolved by the precedent of *War and Peace*: for Tolstoy, the great world-historical figures of Napoleon and his marshals, Koutousov and Alexander I, are included in the novel to demonstrate the vanity of history itself. The inclusion of Alexander I and the future Nicholas I in *Les Compagnons du coquelicot* can be based on their historical importance only. In other words, in *La Lumière des justes*, as to a certain extent in the subsequent Russian *romans-fleuves*, the fictional freedom of the literary text is constrained by the factual, sometimes exotic, historical detail.

Les Eygletière

After *La Lumière des justes* there is a perceptible reduction in the range of Troyat's novel cycles: henceforth he deals with smaller casts of characters and either reduced time-scales or more limited situations within the context of three-volume series. The length and scope of *Tant que la terre durera*, *Les Semailles et les moissons*, and *La Lumière des justes* are not repeated in the subsequent works, a fact conveyed immediately by *Les Eygletière*, which describes the collapse of a contemporary Parisian bourgeois family. The first volume, *Les Eygletière* (1965), shows the family at the beginning of the crisis: the father, Philippe, the rich head of a law firm, sensual and egotistical, and his second wife, the young and beautiful Carole; his children, Jean-Marc, a law student preparing to take his place in the family firm, Daniel, the charming but irresponsible *lycéen*, obsessed by a project to spend the summer in Africa, and Françoise, the pious student at the Ecole des Langues Orientales. On the sidelines, as *confidente*, is the beloved aunt, Madeleine, who lives in comfortable seclusion in her antique shop near Deauville. The situation deteriorates with a precise inevitability: the pious Françoise is lured away from her insipid fiancé and begins a tumultuous affair with her Russian teacher, Alexandre Kozlov; Philippe grows tired of Carole and neglects her, while she declares her love for his son, Jean-Marc. The novel ends with a postponement of the tragedy with Daniel leaving for Africa, Jean-Marc breaking with Carole and fleeing to America, and with a suicide attempt by Françoise.

La Faim des lionceaux (The hunger of the young lions, 1966) continues the family's descent. Françoise decides to cease fighting her love for Kozlov and returns to marry him. Daniel comes back from the Ivory Coast, but a paralyzing lethargy begins to dominate him and he is unable to complete the report which will win him a second journey to Africa. He drifts into an impossible teenage marriage with his pregnant girl friend, Danielle Sauvelot. The main drama, however, is reserved for Jean-Marc. He returns from the United States determined to have nothing to do with Carole, works hard at his studies, and begins to pay court to the wealthy Valérie de Charneray. A vengeful servant informs Philippe of his wife's infidelity, however, and he immediately severs all relations with Jean-Marc. The novel ends with the departure of Carole and the unexpected arrival in the minute apartment of Françoise and Alexandre of Kozlov's illegitimate son, Nicolas.

La Malandre (The faulty beam, 1967) completes the family's downfall. Kozlov makes a journey to Russia and decides to remain there, leaving Françoise and Nicolas alone. Daniel and Danielle have a daughter and install themselves in unthinking vegetation in the family's apartment in the rue Bonaparte. Jean-Marc, still disinherited by his father, becomes engaged to Valérie without much conviction but is strongly drawn to a young student whom he tutors, Gilbert. Finally, Gilbert takes Jean-Marc for a drive in his new sports car, confesses his love for him, and, with Jean-Marc's refusal to run away, deliberately wrecks the car so that they are both killed. Philippe is left alone with Daniel, who lacks his father's willpower, and Carole, who has returned to him but whom he no longer loves. His only object of affection, Jean-Marc, is now dead and life is now distasteful to him: he commits suicide. The cycle ends with Françoise marrying Jean-Marc's best friend Didier, and with Tante Madeleine alone with her antiques.

Troyat sets out his ambitions for the novel in *Un si long chemin:* "C'est l'histoire de la lente désagrégation d'une famille. . . . . Les

fatigues de l'âge mûr opposées au triomphal appétit des jeunes, les
trépidations de la vie moderne, les sourds craquements de la char-
pente sociale vieillie, pourrie, pleine de 'malandres', tels sont les
thèmes essentiels de mon roman" ("It is the story of the slow breakup of a family. . . . The tiredness of middle age set against the
triumphant appetite of the young, the anxieties of modern life, the
creaking of an old rotting social structure, full of faulty beams: these
are the essential themes of my novel," 193).

The problem, however, is that these ambitions are hardly fulfilled
by the novel itself. The battle of the generations, on which Troyat
sets so much store by titling one of the volumes *La Faim des lionceaux,*
is hardly born out in the narrative. Philippe's description of his
children: "Ce sont des lionceaux, durs, coriaces, cruels, égoïstes!"[13]
("They are young lions, hard, tough, cruel, and selfish") matches
imperfectly with the depiction of the vague and irresponsible Daniel,
Françoise in the midst of her emotional turmoil, and Jean-Marc,
the faithful student who is more seduced than seducer. If Philippe's
position is threatened by his children at all, it is through a mild
financial parasitism but emphatically not through an outright attempt to overthrow or supplant him. Indeed, if Philippe commits
suicide, it is largely because of the insipid, unaggressive qualities
in what remains of his family. What has occurred in the novel is a
serious gap between the rhetoric of the narrator and the facts of the
narrative, a gap which ultimately impairs the credibility of the work
as a whole.

A further problem concerns the desire to show the "slow breakup
of a family," for, within the time-scale of the novel, the breakup
is anything but slow. Rather, it is unjustifiably rapid: that a period
of eighteen months to two years should see the infidelity of Jean-
Marc and Carole, Françoise's two marriages, with an attempted
suicide, the marriage of Daniel and the birth of his child, and the
deaths of Jean-Marc and Philippe, carries the work to the point of
implausibility. Nor, as a family novel, does *Les EyGletière* provide
any evidence for the family's rapid collapse: the stupidity of the
children's mother and the moral bankruptcy of Philippe are adduced
as implicit reasons for the downfall, a downfall which, in the end,
is limited to the head of the family and his eldest son.

By attempting to create an illusory period of crisis in the life of
the Eygletières, Troyat has discarded a vital principle of the family-
novel, namely that, in order to be credible, it must show the

evolution of the family through more than one generation. Thus the disintegration of Mann's Buddenbrooks takes place over three generations, ending with the sickly artistic child, Hanno, and Galsworthy similarly depicts the fortunes of the Forsytes from the grandfather, Old Jolyon, to the generation born just before World War I. Even though Duhamel's *La Chronique des Pasquier* covers only two generations, it nevertheless exists in a broad time-scale, from the childhood of the narrator Laurent to his respected middle age. By compressing his action into such a short time span, Troyat has broken the pact with the reader of the *roman-fleuve* by which an equation is established between reading time and narrative time, and is left with the superficiality which is the material of the popular novel.

Nor is the novel raised from this level by the obvious calquing of the action on to the Phaedra myth. Troyat refrains from explicit reference to the myth but is careful to use it implicitly. When writing, in *La Faim des lionceaux,* of Philippe's discovery of Carole's adultery with Jean-Marc, he concludes: "Il se croyait un héros de tragédie grecque" ("He saw himself as a Greek tragic hero," 244). The equation of Philippe-Theseus, Carole-Phaedra, and Jean-Marc-Hippolytus is an overly obvious device in an already unsubtle novel. It is no more effective than the 1961 Jules Dassin film of *Phaedra,* in which the original tragedy is transposed into the world of Greek oil tycoons: the tragic calque is not sufficient to redeem and carry an unconvincing narrative and, indeed, can even serve to emphasize the superficiality of the plot. Moreover, the presence of the Phaedra legend in the novel conflicts with the narrative in that the events are technically by no means tragic because the characters themselves lack tragic status. The suicide of Philippe is not the result of a tragic flaw or the power of destiny, rather the logical and fitting conclusion of a cynical and materialistic life; the death of Jean-Marc is an absurd accident, but not a grandiose punishment; and by transforming Carole from the doomed victim of the Gods into a calculating opportunist, Troyat retains the novel on a superficial level.

In some respects, this is unfortunate. *Les Eygletière* is convincing in its portrait of the lonely aunt Madeleine and the sympathetic concern it shows for the disorientated younger generation just before May 1968. Yet these are minor qualities in a novel which is a failure. Troyat has chosen to depict the world of the upper bourgeoisie which he knows imperfectly and which seems to derive from the fiction of Françoise Sagan. Instead, he has relied upon superficial details which rapidly become the clichés of popular fiction: the rich apartment, the business trips to America, the young wife and the old husband, the fast cars, and the Greek cruises. The decor becomes all-important and psychological action is replaced by melodrama. Refusing the time-scale necessary to a serious family novel and unable to establish the tragic credentials of his characters, Troyat, in *Les Eygletière*, comes as close as he ever does to the transitory, superficial world of the commercial novel.

Les Héritiers de l'avenir

In his next work of extended fiction, however, Troyat draws back from the dangerous world of contemporary popular stereotypes and turns again to the history of nineteenth-century Russia, completing the cycle which runs chronologically from *La Lumière des justes* to the end of *Tant que la terre durera*. Having dealt with the effect of French liberal ideas on Russia at the beginning of the century, leading to the Decembrist uprising, and with the ultimate result, in the form of the two 1917 revolutions, he now describes the major political event in mid-century Russia, the liberation of the serfs under Alexander II. He choses to do this by concentrating on the narrow relationship between a nobleman, Vissarion Variaguine, and his servant, Klim Baranoff, a name possibly inspired by Gorki's *Vie de Klim Sanguine,* which appeared in French translation in 1936.

The first volume, *Le Cahier* (The notebook, 1968), shows Klim as the valued personal servant of the "barine," Vassili Petrovitch Variaguine, who grows up with the master's son, the "bartchouk," Vissarion. Before he dies, Vassili Petrovitch sends Klim as valet to his son in Moscow and orders him to protect and care for the "bartchouk," an order which becomes a sacred injunction for the rest of Klim's life. In Moscow, Vissarion is drawn between the rich and irresponsible conservative students and the serious liberal, Stiopa Plastounoff. While his fortune lasts, he gravitates toward the former, but he gradually loses his money in extravagance and gambling and falls more under the sway of the penniless Stiopa. The volume ends with Vissarion losing Klim at cards to the wealthy landowner Sorokine, ironically in 1859, the very year of the czar's proposal to abolish serfdom, and with Klim seeking consolation in the diary he has kept for four years and which serves as a major component of the narrative.

Cent un coups de canon (A hundred-and-one gun salute, 1969) opens with the once-united Sorokine household squabbling over the sums due to them as their newly awarded payment. The relationship of trust and responsibility between master and serf is now poisoned by the introduction of money. The novel then moves to the family estate of Kossynka where Sorokine, because of his liberalism, is made "arbitre de la paix" for the region, with the task of ensuring an equitable distribution of the land to the peasants. His colleagues among the nobility do not share his liberalism, however, and Sorokine is assassinated while out riding. This leaves Klim without employment and he moves back to Moscow, to his old trade of masseur in a bathing establishment. Here he is about to be married to the owner's daughter when Vissarion and Stiopa arrive in secret, attempting to escape from the police after being implicated in the 1861 assassination attempt on Alexander II. Klim immediately abandons his comfortable post, and the group, including Stiopa's mistress, Ida, sets off through Russia to politicize the peasantry. In so doing, they meet up with a group of liberal students engaged on the same task. Constantly denounced by the very peasants they are trying to help, they end up in Nijny-Novgorod, where Ida dies of typhoid and severs Stiopa's links with humanity. The scene now shifts back to Moscow and St. Petersburg, where Vissarion and Stiopa, followed by the faithful Klim, have moved to the extreme left by becoming members of a terrorist group. In a burlesque episode which reflects the attempt of the terrorist Tchen to kill Chiang Kai Shek, in Malraux's *La Condition humaine*, Vissarion contrives to murder a general's aide-de-camp rather than the general himself. A mistake by Klim leads to the group's arrest and they are awaiting sentence in the Peter and Paul fortress when the hundred-and-one gun salute of the title, which signifies the death of a czar, is heard. It is 1881, and Alexander II has finally been assassinated.

With *L'Eléphant blanc* (1970), Troyat covers the period from 1909 to 1914, with flashbacks to the intervening years by means of Klim's *cahiers*. After the murder of the czar, all revolutionaries were strictly dealt with and Vissarion, Stiopa, and Klim are sent to Siberia. After some years they manage to escape and travel through Japan and America to Paris, where they settle as permanent exiles. Troyat depicts their life and decline with sympathy: their attempt to earn

money by making umbrellas, the heady unreal world of the Russian
émigrés, now split into Social Revolutionaries (terrorists) and Social
Democrats (Mensheviks and Bolsheviks), their increasing irrelevance, their petty bickering, and, finally, their deaths: Stiopa first,
then Vissarion, leaving Klim alone with his umbrellas.

The novel cycle as a whole is one of the most successful works
that Troyat has produced, and *L'Eléphant blanc* in particular deserves
far more attention than it has so far received. Negatively, the cycle
owes its success to the absence of elements which have tended to
mar previous novels: the overdramatized and psychologically im-
plausible depiction of sexual relationships and an undue emphasis
on the superficial exoticism of historical location. Instead, he had
exploited a genuinely tragic theme which subordinates historical
detail to its own abstract connotations, that of the "héritiers de
l'avenir" themselves. When describing Vissarion's tentative con-
version to opposition, Troyat writes: "Il est contre les usages, avec
l'immense majorité de la jeunesse intellectuelle russe. 'Un héritier
de l'avenir!' comme dit Stiopa. Vive Herzen! Vive Ogareff! Vive
Bakounine!"[14] ("He is against present customs, like the vast majority
of young Russian intellectuals. He will 'inherit the future,' as Stiopa
says"). The personal tragedy of Vissarion is that he becomes a revolutionary largely by accident, by moving away from his estate and
losing his money, and that the price he pays in terms of destitution,
imprisonment, and exile is out of all proportion to his initial choices.
The tragedy of his generation is that, even more than the Decembrists, they are made to feel conscious of their role as useful, but
now discarded, precursors of the Revolution, rather than as active
participants. By age, they are denied the Revolution, as Moses is
denied Israel; by conviction, as terrorists rather than as organizers,
they are excluded from the prevailing sense of history.

At the same time, the novel is enriched by the subtle depiction
and analysis of the relationship between Vissarion and Klim, a
relationship which is so close that it appears at times as if only one
personality with different components is being explored. Troyat
sensitively portrays Klim's unending loyalty to his "bartchouk" and
his literal interpretation of his master's trust, maintained in the face
of Vissarion's selfishness. The crucial factor in the relationship,
however, is the interdependence of Vissarion and Klim. Vissarion
needs his servant not merely to survive physically, though it is Klim
who is the breadwinner throughout the novel, but to establish links

with the real world and the past. In his turn, Vissarion is essential to Klim as a reason for existence based upon moral values, again rooted in the past, rather than upon money. For this reason, even when destitute and in flight with Vissarion, he is more secure than when a highly paid servant with Sorokine.

Clearly, the relationship becomes a paradigm of Russian society, by which the nobility and the peasantry are one and need each other in order to exist and have value. With the breaking of the old Russian social contract, both elements become alienated and confused. It is perhaps for this reason that Alexander II occupies a special place in Troyat's thought: the liberation of the serfs appeals to Troyat's liberalism but entails a social fragmentation never to be repaired and which paves the way for the Revolution. This conservative nostalgia for a stable Russian society is intermingled, in the relationship between Vissarion and Klim, with a now familiar pessimistic view of the unchangeable nature of the human psyche: in spite of the momentous events of the novel, Klim remains Vissarion's serf and the irony of his fate lies in the fact that he becomes and lives as a revolutionary from unbending adherence to feudal values, and he never discards his love of the czar or his Orthodox faith. Similarly, the revolutionary intellectual Vissarion, who in point of fact is by no means as intellectual as he would wish to appear, while preaching revolution and equality, continues to maintain an aristocratic distance between himself and Klim and oppresses him as brutally as any preliberation landowner.

What adds further density to the text, however, and alters the balance of the relationship between Klim and Vissarion, is the presence within the novel of Klim's journal, the *cahier* of the first volume. This presence has two immediate effects: it establishes Klim as an autonomous, important character who provides a complementary and often alternative point of view to that of the main narrative dealing with Vissarion and Stiopa; it also permits Troyat to convey economically information through Klim's narrative which would disrupt the movement of the novel if included in the main text. The recounting of the exile in Siberia is a case in point.

What is important, however, is that through his writing Klim establishes a dominance denied him in the relationship with Vissarion and Stiopa. In the first place, whereas the two revolutionaries remain fixed in the positions they adopt at the end of the first volume, Klim, through his reading and the evolution and increasing

sophistication of his style over the three novels, is shown to be the
only one of the three characters to grow in wisdom and sensitivity.
This prepares him for the crucial role in *L'Eléphant blanc*, in which
his diaries, previously hidden from Vissarion and Stiopa, now become essential to their recollection of the past. Like the young man
in *Monsieur Citrine*, Klim has become their memory and, at the same
time, their chronicler who rivals the narrator of the novel himself.
In this respect at least, the roles of master and servant are finally
inverted and Klim gains an unspoken revenge for his status throughout the novel of eternal scapegoat. For this reason, with the death
of Vissarion, he can cease writing.

These complex elements are admirably condensed in the final
volume of the trilogy, *L'Eléphant blanc*. There are few better depic-
tions, save in the novels of Jorge Semprun or Resnais's film *La
Guerre est finie*, of which Semprun wrote the scenario, of the ambiguous pathetic world of the political exile. It is a pathos different
in essence and more acute than that of the émigrés in *Tant que la
terre durera*, where the problem is a passive one of adaptation to a
new environment and hope that circumstances will change through
external forces.

The tragedy of the political exile is that he is actively working
for that change of circumstances, but with imperfect and puny means
because he is operating at a remove from the real field of action.
For this reason, whereas the revolutionary in his homeland is dealing
with the concrete tools of political action—bombs, arms, strikes,
clandestine organization—the exile, all too often, must be content
with the reflection of such activity in the form of lectures, meetings,
and news sheets. In other words, he is left with the rhetoric of
revolution with none of the access to power. In the case of Vissarion
and Stiopa, this situation is rendered more artificial by the passing
of time which not only affects their capacities for action but inevitably allows their ideology to be superseded. The change in Russian
society will not be brought about by the rump of the old Social
Revolutionaries, but by World War I, which begins as the novel
ends, and by the careful exploitation of it by the Social Democrats.
A useful contrast to the irrelevant revolutionaries in *L'Eléphant blanc*
is provided by Solzhenitsyn's novel *Lenin in Zurich* which, by its
concentration upon the Bolshevik leader's ruthless care for organization and the rapid employment of events, shows up the truly
chimerical nature of Vissarion's ambitions.

This outdated quality of the Russian émigrés in the late 1900s is conveyed in the image which gives the novel its title, but which encompasses the psychological pettiness and pathos of Vissarion. Living in a crowded, squalid room with Stiopa and Klim, the aristocrat constantly beneath Vissarion's character is offended, and dreams of luxury. He has already developed a secret childish passion for rum babas, which he indulges each time he delivers a consignment of umbrellas. On one such visit to the umbrella shop, he comes across a magnificent white bathtub and determines to have it, even though it means considerable expenditure from the collective funds. Troyat lovingly describes the long ridiculous journey across Paris, with the serf Klim dragging the tub on a rickety cart, its installation in the apartment which has no plumbing, Vissarion's initial joy and Stiopa's rage at the acquisition, and the bathtub's inevitable neglect. In this one extended image, Troyat is able to convey the outmoded nature of the revolutionaries who have outlived their purpose, Vissarion's aristocratic pretensions and Klim's unalterable status as serf, the beginnings of Vissarion's descent into senile self-indulgence, and the way in which the comradely relationship with Stiopa degenerates into petty warfare. Above all, it is an image which humanely conveys the sense of incongruity, poignancy, and tragedy on which the novel is based.

Le Moscovite

Les Héritiers de l'avenir owes its considerable success to its ability to create complex patterns of profound meaning from a simple but original base. *Le Moscovite* fails because it raises only one major abstract problem, that of dual nationhood, and relies for its narrative effect upon historical details, exoticism, and stereotyped emotional relationships. Moreover, it shows the limits of Troyat's ability to constantly renew the genre of the *roman-fleuve,* in that he is now obliged to repeat conflicts and situations found in the earlier novels.

The first volume, *Le Moscovite* (1974), shows the hero, Armand de Croué, a young French aristocrat who has fled with his father to Russia after the French Revolution and has been received into the home of the wealthy Béreznikoff family. His calm life in the world of the Moscow nobility is disrupted by Napoleon's advance of 1812 and the decision of the Russian high command to abandon the capital after the Battle of Borodino. Paul Arkadievitch Béreznikoff decides

to leave for his estate at Vladimir, accompanied by his wife Nathalie
Ivanovna and his daughter Catherine, but Armand's father refuses
to retreat and Armand remains with him in Moscow, not before he
has received, however, a disturbing embrace from his adoptive
mother.

The arrival of the French is preceded by the death of the old de
Croué from grief and by the burning of Moscow which destroys the
magnificent Béreznikoff house. Armand wanders through the dev-
astated city and, in search of food and shelter, falls in with a group
of French actors and in particular their star, the beautiful Pauline
Filardy, with whom he has a passionate affair. With the establishment of the French army, some normality returns to Moscow and
the theater company are invited to mount performances for the
occupying forces. Armand is caught up in this theatrical life and
ends up by assuming the name of Beaurivage and playing opposite
Pauline in Le Jeu d l'amour et du hasard, a title which points to the
two major elements of the novel's plot. Armand's position becomes
even more ambiguous, however, when, as a Frenchman with perfect
knowledge of Russian, he is pressured by the French administrator
de Lesseps into working as an interpreter for the collaborationist
Moscow City Council and as an agent for supplying the city with
food from the surrounding countryside. The danger of his position
is brought home to him when the French prepare to retreat and he
is informed that, if he remains in Moscow, he faces punishment as
a collaborator. He decides to leave with Pauline and the rest of the
actors.

Les Désordres secrets (Secret turmoils, 1974) continues the description of the retreat from Moscow and shows Armand succumbing to
the cold and hunger and being abandoned by Pauline and the French.
He is saved by the Russian advance, however, and brought home
to the Béreznikoff estate. There, he discovers that his patron Paul
Arkadievitch has died, and he is able to fulfill the promise of his
earlier fleeting embrace with Nathalie Ivanovna, much to the scandal
of the servants and Catherine. His plans to return with Nathalie
Ivanovna to Moscow and rebuild the town house are thwarted by
his arrest and imprisonment as a traitor during the French occupation. Although Nathalie Ivanovna is able to use her influence to
have him released, he remains a political pariah and decides to move
for a time, with his mistress and her daughter, to newly liberated
Paris.

The final volume, *Les Feux du matin* (The lights of morning, 1975), replaces one occupation by another and depicts the restoration, imposed by the Allies, of Louis XVIII. The relationship with Nathalie Ivanovna, who has become dedicated to social success in Paris, deteriorates, especially when Catherine falls ill with tuberculosis and Armand discovers that it is really she whom he loves. Nathalie Ivanovna's jealousy turns to grief and hatred when her daughter dies and she returns to Russia just as Napoleon escapes from Elba. The restitution of Napoleonic power during the Hundred Days sees Armand as a political outcast once more, and he is imprisoned as a traitor and an agent of Russia. Although he is released after Waterloo, his life is now without meaning and when he is killed by drunken Cossacks and his body thrown into the Seine, his death is almost welcome.

The novel has a powerful subject to develop, that of the man who, belonging to two nations, is a citizen of neither. Armand remains French for his Russian friends, while being called "mon petit Moscovite"[15] by Pauline. Distrusted by both nations in times of crisis, the ambiguity of his position is signified by his role as an actor, a favorite image of Troyat's, his participation in the Marivaux play constructed on disguise, and his assumption of a false name. His death in Paris at the hands of the troops of his adoptive country is the product of a logical inevitability. At the same time, Armand's activities in Moscow under Napoleonic rule point to a careful reflection on Troyat's part on the complexity of collaboration: Armand enters into it as the result of accident, his being in the wrong place at the wrong time, intimidation, and the promise that his work, without benefiting the occupier, will save the lives of the native population. It is as if Troyat has taken arguments used by the defense in the *Haute Cour* following the Liberation and has transposed them into the Napoleonic period. In so doing, he has undoubtedly given to his work a broader significance, as well as participating in the renewed debate on the Occupation which arose in the 1970s and was concentrated in France on the controversy surrounding Bertolucci's film *The Night Porter* and Louis Malle's *Lacombe Lucien*.

The problem, however, is that Troyat adds little to what he has written or implied in earlier works. The question of dual nationality is broached with Boris Danoff, in *Etrangers sur la terre* and is continued in *La Rencontre*. More precisely, *Le Moscovite* covers problems amply dealt with in *La Lumière des justes,* in which the Russian occupation of Paris plays a large part at the beginning and where Sophie, French by birth but Russian by marriage, experiences the same alienation in both countries. Similarly, both *Les Compagnons du coquelicot* and *Sophie ou la fin des combats* pose the question of chauvinist intolerance in times of crisis and the way in which Sophie's private commitment to Nicolas and her political commitment to liberalism are, in both countries and at different times, given sinister treasonable implications. In other words, to a large extent Troyat is failing to find new themes for his long fictional works and is obliged to repeat and concentrate on existing ones. This would not be so serious if the novel were able to raise other abstract concerns, but in this respect it is considerably impoverished.

In time-scale it stands at the beginning of Troyat's Russian cycles, but outside their concerns. The burning of Moscow and the Allied occupation of Paris have significance here only in the context of Armand's dual nationality: they do not appear, as they do in *La Lumière des justes,* as the beginning of a process of radicalization in Russia which will end with the Revolution. The novel is cut off from the thematic significance of *La Lumière des justes, Les Héritiers de l'avenir,* and *Tant que la terre durera,* and historical events are exotic details which assist the plot and not the springboard for abstract concern.

This has the effect of conferring a lightness upon *Le Moscovite* which comes dangerously close to slightness. The reduction in abstract weight is compensated for by concentration upon the three love affairs which make up the bulk of the narrative, an area of fictional representation in which Troyat does not excel. Armand's affair with the actress Pauline is convincing, but only because it is conventional and expected. Its credibility is retained retrospectively by Pauline's realism and self-seekingness, when she abandons Armand during the retreat from Moscow for the rich Muffelet-Colard, and recognizes that their later meeting in Paris has been a failure.

The triangular relationship with Nathalie Ivanovna and Catherine, however, loses that credibility. In creating Nathalie Ivanovna, Troyat has built on the Phaedra connotations of the relationship between Carole and Jean-Marc in *Les Eyglétière,* but has attempted to infuse his heroine with a tragic tension between passion and pious guilt which she, as a character, is unable to bear. All too frequently, the reponse evoked in the reader is the same as that felt by Armand, irritation rather than pity. With Catherine, Troyat has similarly created a conventional character, that of the true love who remains temporarily obscured by a passing passion. Also, in her early disdain for Armand's affair with her mother, Troyat borrows a character trait from Sophie, in *Les Compagnons du coquelicot.* Yet the mutual declaration of love of Armand and Catherine is so predictable and so delayed that it lacks dramatic impact, and Catherine's subsequent death maintains the novel in its conventional popular modes by exploiting a fund of sentimentality.

If *Les Héritiers de l'avenir* shows the way in which Troyat can manipulate the *roman-fleuve* to admirable and important literary effect, *Le Moscovite* demonstrates the dangers which the genre holds. An overreliance on one theme, with a disproportionate attention devoted to exotic historical detail and the sentimental life of the characters, can imply a thinness of the novel as a whole and an almost inevitable use of the conventions of popular fiction. For this reason, an easy distinction can be operated between those novels whose titles indicate abstract preoccupations—*Tant que la terre durera, Les Semailles et les moissons, La Lumière des justes,* and *Les Héritiers de l'avenir*—and those concentrated on individuals or families—*Les Eygletière* and *Le Moscovite*—where manipulation of plot and psychological investigation dominate.

Nevertheless, Troyat's use of the genre indicates certain preoccupations and implications common to both types of novel. All, to a greater or lesser extent, demonstrate a fatalistic view of the vulnerability and powerlessness of the individual in the face of historical movements or even psychological impulsions. It is for this reason that the anguished question, "Qu'allons-nous devenir?" ("What is to become of us?") echoes as a leitmotiv throughout the long novels, a leitmotiv which tends to establish itself as a cliché of melodrama. This underlying fear of historical movement, however, with the compensatory vigorous defense of individual happiness, is translated into a certain implicit political stance by which bourgeois values are celebrated and defended against the forces which threaten them. It is no coincidence, for example, the *Tant que la terre durera* and *Les Semailles et les moissons* present a highly favorable depiction of the work ethic, by which Michel and Tania rise to riches initially through hard work and judicious investment and finally reestablish themselves in France through the same modest values. Similarly, Amélie and Pierre are able to rise through an application of the same values from the rural peasantry to the Parisian petite bourgeoisie and then

to the hotel-owning bourgeoisie, while their daughter Elizabeth has
gravitated from the original family home in Montmartre to the
fashionable rue François Ier.

At the same time, Troyat is conscious of the forces undermining
this social structure. At the beginning of his study of the idyllic
final period of the Russian Empire, *La Vie quotidienne en Russie au
temps du dernier tsar,* he comments that, after 1904, the situation
deteriorated dramatically: "Sous son apparente stabilité administrative, elle cachait un malaise, une angoisse, qui devait aboutir aux
tragiques événements de 1917"[16] ("Beneath its apparent administrative stability, the regime concealed a malaise, an anxiety, which
were to result in the tragic events of 1917"). The origins of this
"malaise" go back to the well-meaning but misguided activities of
the Decembrists who, for Troyat, triggered off the whole irreversible
revolutionary process. Through the characters of *La Lumière des justes,*
he points to the personal futility of political action, the wasted lives,
but also to the way in which it conjures up dark forces which become
uncontrollable. The Decembrists lead to the assassins of Alexander
II, who lead in their turn to the Social Democrats who will make
the Revolution and eradicate the old order. It is for this reason that
the "liberal" Czar Alexander II occupies such a pivotal position in
Troyat's thought: the head of state able to guide Russia into the
modern era while preserving the social structure, perversely assassinated by those who agreed with his policies but nevertheless condemned them in the name of a higher political passion. It is this
passion which is dangerous in the extended fiction, for it removes
the characters from the ordinary humane scheme of things to a realm
where they can do immense damage.

Nor is the bourgeois edifice menaced only by external forces, it
is being undermined from within. *Les Héritiers de l'avenir* shows the
younger generation playing at revolution by converting the peasants
to social change, a game which, as the years pass, becomes in deadly
earnest. Similarly, in *Les Eygletière,* the moral bankruptcy of the
older generation, which constitutes one of the "malandres," is mirrored by the irresponsibility and restiveness of their children which
announce the political upheavals of May 1968. If the dynamic tension of Troyat's long fiction, therefore, is between the preservation
of bourgeois values and a vision of their collapse, he has chosen to
adopt a fictional mode which reinforces the values which he wishes
to defend. The solidity, the self-confidence, the traditionalism of

the *roman-fleuve* serve as an implicit defense against the revolutionary values without and doubt and corruption within. Thus, whereas *L'Eléphant blanc* is a political novel of a high standard, its traditional narration, even with the inclusion of Klim's journal, reflects its distrust of the extremist activities of the protagonists; Jorge Semprun's scenario for *La Guerre est finie* or his novel, *La Deuxième mort de Ramon Mercader,* by their very disruption and dislocation of traditional narrative, introduce a revolutionary, contestatory perspective.

Troyat's long novels, therefore, like his short fiction, remain determined to a large extent by the properties of the genres themselves. Significantly, his apparently most spectacular escape from these constraints is to be found in a genre where the Russian influence is the most clear, the novellas and short stories.

Chapter Five
Short Stories and Novellas

When Troyat's collection of two novellas, "La Clef de voûte" and "Monsieur Citrine," was published in 1937, the critical reaction was immediately of a different order from that which greeted the early novels. While Marcel Arland's conclusion, in the *Nouvelle Revue Française*, attempts a general description of Troyat's literary preoccupations—"Ce qui touche le plus chez M. Troyat et semble à la base de son inspiration, c'est un goût, un sens des maladies de l'âme, des déchéances, de la dépossession d'un être"[1] ("The most touching aspect of Troyat's work and what seems to be the basis of his inspiration is a taste for and a sense of spiritual sickness, decline, and the deprivation of a human being")—his criticism of the unsubtle evocation of these themes is plainly more appropriate to the novels than to the short stories.[2] These, in contrast, are "apparentées par un goût de l'anormal, de l'étrange, presque du monstrueux, et plus encore par le rythme de leur allure"[3] ("they are related in their taste for the abnormal, for the strange, almost for the unnatural, and even more by their rhythm") and, while Arland stops short of claiming that "le domaine véritable de M. Henri Troyat est la fantaisie"[4] ("the real area of M. Henri Troyat is the fantastic"), it is an implied distinction between the novels and the short stories which grows more relevant as Troyat continues to explore the genre of the *nouvelle*. This distinction is also reinforced by Troyat's own comment in *Un si long chemin* that his short stories "étaient pour moi une sorte de récréation pleine de folie au milieu du cours régulier de mes travaux" ("a form of whimsical recreation from my regular work," 73). Paradoxically, it is precisely this liberation from what he sees as the mainstream of his literary production which results in some of Troyat's most rewarding and neglected writing: the two collections of novellas, *La Clef de voûte* (1937) and *Le Jugement de Dieu* (1941), together with three volumes of short stories, *La Fosse commune* (1939), *Du Philanthrope à la Rouquine* (From the philanthropist to the redhead, 1945) and *Le Geste d'Eve* (1964).[5]

It is this strain of his work, which runs parallel to the novels, *romans-fleuves,* and biographies and retains its own separate thematic and stylistic properties, which constitutes Troyat's most original contribution to French prose fiction. Of all his work, it is the novellas and short stories which show the greatest awareness of literary context and literary tradition, from the Flaubertian stylization of history in *Le Jugement de Dieu* to the world of Hoffmann and Gogol which informs the short stories. In this way, Troyat is able to introduce a new tone into his prose writing, by which the domination of psychological or historical causality, which so often constrains his novels and *romans-fleuves,* gives way to a development of the fantastic. Through the concentration on the Devil figure of Gogol's *Evenings on a Ukrainian Farm* and a subtle use of the folktale, in "L'Ame de Mélitone" (The soul of Mélitone), "Le Ratuset," and "Le Sortilege" (The spell), he is able to construct the same disquieting atmosphere as that which pervades Julien Gracq's *La Presqu'île,* arrived at from the direction of French surrealism. At the same time, because of the necessarily compressed nature of the writing, Troyat's short stories achieve a textual density and self-reflexiveness largely absent from his other work which contribute to their artistic complexity and stature. In this context it is no accident that these properties should coincide with the fact that the short stories represent Troyat's only excursion into a fundamentally noncommercial literary genre.[6]

La Clef de voûte

The volume comprising the two novellas "La Clef de voûte" and "Monsieur Citrine" was published in 1937 but, as Troyat reminds the reader of *Un si long chemin,* the first story appeared some years earlier in the *Revue Hebdomadaire* and constitutes his first serious fictional work. This fact in itself goes some way toward explaining Marcel Arland's differing reactions to the two stories, by which he sees the former as considerably inferior to the latter. In this respect, the volume is useful in the way in which it isolates the point at which Troyat's fiction is able to depart from purely psychological constraints by exploiting fully the properties of the *nouvelle.* "La Clef de voûte" is still part of Troyat's apprenticeship and presents stronger affinities with his other writing of the 1930s than the more original "Monsieur Citrine." At the same time, it has very real qualities which already remove it from the world of the novels. The story is written in the first person, in the form of a diary, a fact which constitutes a fruitful departure for Troyat and allows him the same benefits as in *Le Mort saisit le vif.* Its narrator, Monsieur Proste, a minor clerk, lives alone with his sister Thérèse whom he dominates. One morning Proste returns for lunch with a headache and, furious that there is no aspirin in the apartment, orders his sister to buy some. A sudden screech of brakes warns him that she has been knocked down and killed while on the errand. Then follows a long exploration of solitary guilt in which readily explicable psychological elements, such as imagined persecution by the neighbors, give way to supernatural ones. Proste becomes aware of his sister's presence in the room as a shadow, imprisoning and torturing him as he once tortured her, and increasing her aggression until she attempts to kill him. The remainder of the *nouvelle* recounts Proste's struggle to exorcise the ghost, an exorcism which amounts to a second murder.

Clearly, "La Clef de voûte" contains elements common to the psychological fiction of the 1930s. Indeed, Troyat recalls in *Un si long chemin* that the paranoid elements in his hero coincide with his interest in psychiatry and the lectures he attended at the Hôpital Sainte-Anne. Similarly, Proste's sense of, first, being reproached by the inhabitants of his *quartier* and then being openly persecuted by them, establishes a common ground between Troyat and the Simenon of *Le Petit homme d'Archangelsk.* More precisely, the relationship between Proste and Thérèse which subtends the entire work is the familar one of claustrophobia and domination which characterizes *L'Araigne* and *Le Vivier.* For this reason, much of the imagery situates the work in the context of the novels: Proste refers to his "honte de mauvais acteur"[7] ("shame of a bad actor") and describes the second death of Thérèse in terms which apply equally to Gérard Fonsèque: "Au centre de cette gluante toile d'araignée, Thérèse étouffait comme une mouche prise" ("In the center of this sticky spider's web, Thérèse suffocated like a captured fly," 102). Nevertheless, the story's preoccupations are profoundly different from those of the novels, a difference heralded by the first-person narration.

"La Clef de voûte" is a reflection on duality, a duality which is both psychological and moral. Proste discovers that his relationship with Thérèse is so close that they are almost part of one personality, like Klim and Vissarion in *Les Héritiers de l'avenir*. Hence, her presence as a shadow is indispensable to his own existence, the keystone of his existence, first threatening, then threatened. His guilt at her death becomes the means of maintaining her as an element in his life. For this reason, the novella becomes naturally a ghost story in which the psychological and supernatural become entwined and where Troyat is able to move from the myth of the shadow who escapes its owner to the absolute legend of the *Doppelgänger*, the double who, when seen, spells death for the protagonist. In this context, both myths may be seen as proceeding from the psychological, in that they describe an exteriorization of guilt and anxiety and a fragmentation of the personality on schizophrenic lines. At the same time, they open the fiction out into a disquieting world in which the normal framework of understanding is no longer applicable.

In this context, it is by no means coincidental that the story appears to derive strongly from Dostoevski's *Notes from the Underground*, as well as from Stevenson's *Doctor Jekyll and Mister Hyde*, to which explicit reference is made (93). Whereas Stevenson proposes a radical split in one personality on moral grounds, Dostoevski uses the duality of above and below ground and the frailty of both conventional morality and the rationalist philosophy of 2 times 2 equals 4 to construct an underground narrator, oscillating between exaggerated guilt and self-abasement and an uncontrollable sense of superiority. Thus, Proste equates the desire to "toucher le fond" ("touch bottom," 91) with the reflection, "Suis-je un monstre? Je ne le crois pas. Simplement un homme fort qui s'ignorait et se découvre" ("Am I a monster? I do not think so. Merely a strong man who was unaware of his strength and who is discovering it," 27), and the entire narrative plays upon the same ambiguity raised by Dostoevski, whether the superiority is merely the rationalization of the abasement or whether the self-abasement and superiority are part of the same rejection of normality in favor of a deeper truth. This ambiguity is compounded by the very falsity of Proste's position: "Non, je ne suis pas un assassin! *Je ne suis même pas un assassin!*" ("No I am not a murderer! *I am not even a murderer!*" 97).

Arland's criticism of the novella is based upon the intrusive nature of its structure, in which moral and psychological duality is reflected in the two characters and repetition in the plot, and upon the determinist role of the unconscious guilt upon the narrative. For

this reason, he refers to its "progression trop rapide et quasi géométrique" ("too rapid and almost geometrical progression") and the
"pénible impression de mécanisme"[8] ("painfully mechanical impression") which it creates. Nevertheless, Troyat is able to allow the
reader considerably more freedom of interpretation than in the novels
and raises issues which go far beyond the depiction of purely psychological domination. The constraints of structure are the result
of the early position of the work in Troyat's production, and by the
time he comes to deal with the same issues in "Monsieur Citrine,"
he has learned a subtlety and lightness of touch which allows the
full ambiguity of the work to appear.

M. Citrine is a rich bachelor living in Troyat's old home of
Neuilly, who suffers from a form of amnesia which prevents him
remembering the day-to-day events of his life, without impairing
his sense of identity. In order to rectify this situation he hires a
memory, the young Jean Piguet whose task is to discreetly follow
his employer throughout the day and to present a report on his
activities. In this way Citrine is reunited with his recent past and
enjoys the comfort of subordinating Piguet to his own life. In time,
however, Citrine discovers that his memory has returned and that
there are serious discrepancies between his own recollections and
Piguet's reports: his employee, tired of being chained to his master,
simply abandons him during the day and invents his report for the
evening. In a rage, Citrine dismisses Piguet and wakes in the morning to discover a letter of resignation from his servant. The shock
of this autonomous text is so great that Citrine collapses, and when
he comes to, his memory has once more vanished.

As Arland comments on the story: "On voit toutes les allusions,
toutes les échappées que comporte une telle histoire. C'est presque
un conte moral, à la manière de Voltaire"[9] ("You can see all the
allusions, all the vistas contained in the story. It is almost a moral
tale, in the manner of Voltaire"). The tale is rich and operates on
both a psychological and textual level, linked by the continued use
of the image of the shadow. The employment of Piguet amounts
to the most extreme form of domination to be found in Troyat's
fiction: the reduction of another being to a physiological function
of the protagonist. Piguet's bizarre employment allows him no freedom and no autonomy: his daylight hours are spent, not on himself,
but chained to the life of his master; his use of language, reasonably
the supreme assertion of personal liberty, is directed solely toward

the daily biography of Citrine. Similarly, Citrine, like the protagonist of *Le Vivier* or Gérard Fonsèque, revels in the imprisonment to the extent that, when his memory has returned, he continues for some time to acquiesce in the fiction and is destroyed by Piguet's final assertion of his independence.

What makes the story so interesting, however, is the way in which Troyat places the relationship between man and existence on a literary, fictional level. Citrine does not merely profit from the subjection of Piguet, he revels in the narration of his own daily life: he becomes the hero of a book ostensibly meant to be a faithful biography but which, revealed to be fictional, becomes even more alluring. In other words, the comfort he derives from Piguet's daily reports is connected with the transfer of his life from a contingent to an aesthetic plane: hence the shock caused, not by Piguet's departure, but by the reading of the letter of resignation which, as a piece of autonomous writing, directed at Citrine rather than using him as a subject, destroys the world of literary biography in which Citrine has been happy to live.

"Monsieur Citrine," therefore, goes far beyond the study of a wealthy neurasthenic with a passion for domination, and is able to operate on a purely textual level, in which different types of writing confront each other. In this way the story is able to open out still further from the subject of the tyrannical employer who wishes to be the sole subject of his servant's writing, to a reflection of the relationship between author and reader in the narrative itself. The use of the symbol of the shadow and the range of mirror imagery contribute to a satisfying freedom in the text, by which the various elements combine and reflect each other to an infinite degree. It is this removal of the limitations of interpretation, which tend to lessen the effect of the rest of Troyat's prose fiction, which enhances the qualities of the two stories and makes the publication of *La Clef de voûte* an important stage in his literary development.

La Fosse commune

La Clef de voûte consists of two novellas, both a hundred pages long, in which Troyat demonstrates his ability to manipulate his material in a careful but relaxed manner and uses a narrative form which is still relatively extended and retains some of the properties of the short novels. In addition, the two novellas are closely inter-

linked, in preoccupation and form, and combine to produce a coherent united volume. In contrast, *La Fosse Commune* is more related
to the nineteenth-century convention of collections of existing stories. Its title, with its connotations of the macabre, confers a certain
unity upon the work, but by no means conveys all the elements in
play. The volume is, rather, an *ad hoc* collection of short stories in
which Troyat temporarily abandons the length and seriousness of
the novellas to experiment with short, compressed narratives, often
ostensibly more occasional and whimsical. The collection therefore
constitutes to some extent a series of *exercices du style* in which the
author demonstrates his ability to manipulate a wide range of subjects and stylistic registers and shows his proficiency in the area of
comedy. At the same time, light as these stories may appear, they
nevertheless continue preoccupations raised in the novellas and,
because of their comic incongruity, lead the reader into a world
which is strange but far from superficial.

The slightest of the stories in *La Fosse commune* is "Le Vertige"
(Vertigo), which deals with Mlle Pascal, the spinsterish head of a
civil service department. Annoyed at the absence of her assistant,
M. Huche, she discovers that he is exhibiting paintings at the
department's annual exhibition and determines to go and see his
work. Once at the exhibition, she is drawn to a collection of semi-
pornographic nudes, only to discover that they bear the signature
of her assistant. There follows a period in which Mlle Pascal passes
from outrage to fascinated speculation on Huche's view of women
in general and of her in particular. She finally plucks up courage
to ask him to paint her portrait, only to be told that the real author
of the paintings is a M. Ruche and that her assistant paints cats.
The gentle comedy of the story, which derives from Troyat's own
role as a writer in the prefecture of the Seine, is based upon the
confusion of names but also, more seriously, on the repressed sexuality of the protagonist. Beneath the humor there lies the sad
portrait of a lonely individual who, like M. Citrine, lives richly
only in an aesthetic reflection of real life.

A more complicated concern is evoked in two stories, "L'Assassin"
(The murderer) and "Le Ressac" (The undertow), in which Troyat
explores the notion of a false causality which he has already developed
in "La Clef de voûte." In "L'Assassin" the narrator meets an old
army colleague, Rameaux, in a bar, and the story consists of Rameaux's recounting of his own peculiar experience. He explains to

the narrator that he had discovered that his wife was unfaithful to him and had laid careful plans to murder her lover. When about to put the plan into operation, he learned that the lover had been run over in the street and killed. Far from feeling relieved, Rameaux feels morally responsible for the death and so determines to leave his wife as if he were genuinely guilty. The story stands midway between "La Clef de voûte," in which Proste, even though innocent, feels responsible for Thérèse's death, and "Le Jugement de Dieu," in which the hero is eternally denied punishment and hence absolution. As Rameaux concludes: "On se repent d'un crime qu'on a commis. Or, j'étais innocent. Je n'avais pas tué. Je n'avais même pas tué. Je n'avais même pas l'excuse d'avoir tué"[10] ("You can repent of a crime you have committed. But I was innocent. I had not killed. I had not even killed. I did not even have the excuse of having killed").

The story adopts for the first time one of the structural characteristics of Troyat's short stories and a dominant element in the fantastic folk-tale: a narrator who mediates between the reader and the extreme experience of the protagonist. Nor can that experience be reduced to a banal feeling of remorse that one's wishes have become fact. The effect of the story lies in the way in which, for Rameaux (ironically named after Palm Sunday, a day of salvation), the wish has, in an almost supernatural way, become concrete, that there is a causal connection between his intention and an apparently unrelated accident. The irony, however, is that, because that connection is only present in Rameaux's mind and not in the legal world, he is condemned to be innocent in a fictional world where values are inverted.

This establishment of a fictional causality is pursued in the last story in the collection, "Le Ressac," in which Jean Dupont, having indifferently broken with his mistress, is accidentally run over. Immediately, a false connection is established between the two events, so that it is generally believed that the accident was a suicide attempt.[11] What is interesting about the story is that Dupont comes to believe it too, to the extent that when his mistress marries, he genuinely commits suicide in despair. Troyat has now introduced a new element into the argument. If the false causality leaves Rameaux, the would-be murderer, in a state of inexpiable innocence, it leaves Dupont, who bears a name of stock comic anonymity, in a situation where the assumption of suicide can only be directed against himself. The connection between suicide attempt and accident is indeed fictitious, but, as for Mlle Pascal and M. Citrine, it provides the only world where he can exist and be defined, even though it will ultimately lead to his self-destruction.

In "L'Assassin" and "Le Ressac" Troyat is interested in coincidence both as the basis for an obsessive feeling of unjustified guilt and as the foundation of an illogical world in which nevertheless his heroes discover a meaning and a grandeur denied them outside it. It is this which constitutes the temptation of false causality, that it constructs a broader scheme of things, a temptation explored more precisely in two further stories, "Erratum" and "La Dame Noire" (The lady in black).

The first goes to the very heart of the problem, the meaning and interpretation of statistics. Alain Laquelle is a professional statistician working in the village of Gabiaule-les-Ponts, who has so perfected his analysis of local mortality rates that he is able to predict them. The local populace rapidly conclude that he is not merely a faithful scientist, but that his weekly predictions constitute a death sentence, a conclusion reached by Laquelle himself when he tries to break the causality by inventing a figure, only to see that figure consistently reached as if by some diabolical power. Eventually, the narrator, a faithful reader of the local newspaper, tries to save Laquelle by giving him the arbitrary number of 118 deaths for the end of the following week. With a few moments to go, it seems as if he has won, for the figure stands at only 117. Rushing to announce the news to his friend, he discovers Laquelle dead in his room, having committed suicide.

The story can be read in two ways. On one level, it demonstrates the same elements present in "Le Ressac": the dangerous link between observation and prediction and the more sinister false connection between prediction and event. Dangerous and false as these connections are, they provide the only justification for Laquelle's existence and, when they appear to fail, he commits suicide. At the same time, a new element enters the narrative: although the reader disdains the peasants' naive interpretations of Laquelle's work, he is skillfully maneuvered by Troyat into believing that the accuracy of the statistician's *random* predictions is not coincidental and can only occur through some supernatural influence.

For the first time, the Devil enters Troyat's fiction and is born in the juxtaposition of events no longer explicable by rational laws.

The same problem is raised in "La Dame Noire," in which the narrator, an author, is staying at a luxury hotel. There, he meets the aged Madame Naude who agrees to tell him a story which will serve as material for his craft. The old lady is ill and scared of dying by herself. For this reason, she has spent the last ten years of her life traveling from hotel to hotel in search of another person near to death under the same roof. If someone dies during her residence at the hotel, she too will die and enter the afterlife with company. Yet, as she wrily admits, her presence serves more as a guarantee of good health for the population of the hotels in which she stays. This confident assertion is contradicted by the news that the porter Eugène has fallen ill. Madame Naude becomes agitated, appears to decline, and the narrator is convinced that she will not last the night. On the following morning, however, he learns that Eugène is dead and that the lady in black has left the hotel. In this story, the coincidence of the old lady's presence and Eugène's fatal illness can be read as nothing other than supernatural, with the narrator acting once again as mediator with the reader. Her protestations of wishing merely to die with another person break down in the light of her sinister, unreal appearance, and her true function becomes apparent, that of a decoy luring others to their death and leaving at the last moment. The supernatural causality is now clear and the short stories now enter the realm of the ghost story.

This genre is represented by two pieces in the collection, one burlesque, "Le Tandem," and one in deadly earnest, "Le Ratuset." The former concerns the Poucide couple, whose joy it is to ride their tandem bicycle around the countryside. M. Poucide dies, however, and his widow prepares to take a lover. But she is out riding the tandem one day when the ghost of her dead husband takes up position behind her and takes control of the bicycle, spiriting her away from the earth.

Slight as the story is, in its comic punishment of projected infidelity and assertion of the continued principle of the couple, it serves as a useful counterpart to the strange and worrying world of "Le Ratuset." Here, Troyat employs the traditional material of the ghost story: a narrator who is a soldier billeted with his three comrades in a lonely barn at night. Waking suddenly at midnight, he overhears two soldiers, Chalicot and Salade, discussing ghosts. Chalicot, a northerner, does not believe in ordinary ghosts, but he does not dispute the existence of "ratusets," the mischievous spirits of his native north. This long scene-setting serves as an introduction to the narrative-within-a-narrative, that recounted by Salade.

When working as a telephone engineer near Dijon, he received a bizarre commission: a Madame Bazaille, terrrifed of being buried alive, insisted on a telephone being placed in her coffin, linking her with her son. Shortly after, she dies, and Salade connects the coffin with a telephone in her son's bedroom. He is awakened the following night by the terrified son, who insists that the telephone has rung. In the graveyard, they find the tomb broken open, with the mother undeniably dead but showing signs of a superhuman struggle. The son breaks down and goes mad, and the narrative shifts back to the present, where, to show the effect of the narrative on the listener, Troyat has the barn door blown open and the terrified Chalicot lapsing into his northern accent and screaming: "Si t'y crois pas, aux ratusets, va vir, va vir, qui ch'est qu'a buqué à ch'porte!"[12] ("If you don't believe in *ratusets,* go and see, go and see who banged the door!").

The story depends for its effect upon the way in which it descends through several levels of narration: the description of the army on the march, the evocation of the old barn, the narrator as eaves-dropper, Chalicot's defense of the existence of "ratusets," all leading finally to the central tale told by Salade, which in itself owes much to Poe's "The Tell-tale Heart." Troyat's skill in manipulating his reader's emotions lies first in the economy and vividness of his scene setting but much more in the way that, even if the extreme horror of Salade's story can be dismissed on rational grounds, there is an irreducible core of the supernatural in the *récit,* centered on the "ratuset." By using two supernatural elements, Troyat makes it difficult for the reader to deny the presence of at least a lesser world beyond the rational, an operation sealed by the slamming of the door and Chalicot's rejection of his formal French for northern *patois.*

If Troyat moves, in *La Fosse commune,* from the purely psychological to the coincidental and ultimately to the ghost story, he ends up in the world of science fiction. The first story in the volume, "Les Cobayes" (The guinea-pigs), relates how Albert Pincelet, a young man about to commit suicide, is saved by Professor Otto Dupont who employs him as a human guinea pig in his experiments on personality changes. While in the laboratory, Pincelet falls in love with another employee, Yolande Vincent. Disturbed by the changes in personality they are undergoing, they decide to escape and lead a normal life, only to discover that life outside the heightened world of the laboratory is too dull. The story ends with their return to Dupont.

The tale takes place in a world of fictional stereotype: Dupont, who looks forward to his namesake in "Le Ressac," is benign but anonymous, calqued on the figure of the experimental scientist found in H. G. Wells or Jules Verne. Nevertheless, Troyat is able to raise an important problem: the relative insipidness of ordinary life in comparison with a heightened world of extreme situations, while affirming, in a rare expression of optimism, the irreducible nature of the human spirit: "Les pîqures du professeur Otto Dupont bouleversaient la surface de l'être, mais la flore sous-jacente, les profondeurs abritées de l'âme, les sources de la chaleur, de la vie, de l'amour, demeuraient certainement intactes" ("Professor Otto Dupont's injections disturbed the surface, but the underlying flora, the preserved depths of the soul, the sources of warmth, life and love, remained definitely intact," 38).

The same atmosphere of science fiction pervades "Mr. Breadborough," a story about an English psychical researcher, who owes much to Conan Doyle's Professor Challenger stories, who has created a stir by resigning from the various psychic bodies. The interviewer sent to find out the truth behind the resignation discovers that Breadborough, investigating psychic presences in a Scottish castle, has killed a ghost by firing a pistol at it, thus proving that spirits are as mortal as humans, merely living out an invisible mortal existence and, after suffering all the pain of human death, are reincarnated in the mortal world. This representation of the spirit world is a particularly fruitful one and looks forward to "Le Guéridon" (The table) and the influence both stories undoubtedly have on Sartre's *Les Jeux sont faits* (1946). More important, it is part of the process of inversion by which Troyat obtains some of his most successful effects: initially, the concept of a mortal ghost is humorous, but the humor gives way to vivid pathos as the death agony of the phantom conveys profoundly the tragedy of any mortality. In this way, the spirit world and the human world are each reflections of the other, with a common denominator in the value of individual existence.

While *La Fosse commune* is obviously not the product of a coherent plan, its stories may be grouped so as to show a certain number of unified preoccupations. Through his explorations of false causality

and coincidence, Troyat is able to create a convincing fictional world
which exists on many levels and in which a metaphysical concern
is evident. Paradoxically, it is these stories of bizarre situations and
an ill-defined malignant influence on the world which permit humor
and humanity to show through whereas they are often stifled by the
psychological oppressiveness of the novels or the historical process
in the *romans-fleuves*.

Le Jugement de Dieu

With *Le Jugement de Dieu* Troyat returns to the extended novella
and reinforces the view that the preoccupations of the short stories
are separate from those of his other work. Significantly, it is the
work which evokes the most clearly a far-off, mythical past, and
which was one of his few works written and published during the
Occupation. As he records in *Un si long chemin,* they allowed him,
like *Tant que la terre durera,* to escape from the misery of the present
into a miraculous past. [13]

The first story in the collection of three, "Le Jugement de Dieu"
itself, opens in a Villonesque depiction of the Middle Ages. An
incorrigible criminal, Alexandre Mirette, is charged with murder
and put to the divine test of being immersed in burning oil. Inex-
plicably, Mirette is saved and his vindication is hailed as a miracle.
A merchant, Taillade, takes him in, and becomes his protector, but
becomes disillusioned upon discovering that Mirette has seduced his
wife, Dame Blanche. Instead, he propounds the theory that Mirette's
deliverance was due, not to the clemency of God, but to a simple
omission and that judgment is still to be rendered. Henceforth,
Mirette finds himself in the same limbo as that inhabited by Proste
and Rameaux, and he sets out on an orgy of crime in order to provoke
the punishment he deserves and which will restore meaning to him.
On each occasion, however, punishment is withheld and Mirette
finally grasps the fact that his real punishment lies in not being
punished. So he goes on through the ages, a Flying Dutchman under
the judgment of God, until he ends up as a parody of himself, a
street entertainer in a flea market burning his feet in oil for the
delight of the crowds.

The attraction of the novella lies in the creation, in Alexandre
Mirette, of an incorrigible rogue in a romanticized medieval setting
akin to that of Carco's *Le Roman de François Villon* (1926). Beneath

this setting, however, lies the fantastic element of the tale, Mirette's condemnation to an eternity in which punishment is withheld, and the paradox by which nonpunishment is more damning that execution. Beyond this reiterated emphasis on the necessity for punishment in order to exorcise guilt, the novella does not develop any further complexity of thought. In this case, in contrast to the subtlety of "La Clef de voûte" and "Monsieur Citrine," the properties of the legend dominate and impose a necessary simplicity and linearity.

The same pattern persists in the second legend, "Le Puy Saint-Clair," set in Tulle on the eve of the Wars of Religion. The story opens with the funeral procession of Catherine Eyrolles, the daughter of a wealthy merchant, followed by her family and her grieving fiancé, the sculptor Lamansarde. Commissioned to build her tomb, the sculptor throws himself into his work with such fervor that a subtle change operates and he becomes more obsessed with the beauty of his sculpture, on the hillside of the Puy Saint-Clair, than with the love that was its origin. His obsession is temporarily interrupted by the attack of Huguenot forces on Tulle, and Lemansarde takes part in the defense of the city. As the battle rages, it moves up the Puy Saint-Clair toward the cemetery, and Lamansarde fights single-handedly to defend his sculpture. By the end of the day, the sculpture is irreparably damaged and Lamansarde is exhausted and goes to sleep, but not before realizing that, with the destruction of the tomb, a spell has been broken and he is now able to love Catherine again. At this, he awakes to discover that Catherine has been returned to him, with the words: "Je ne pouvais pas revenir à toi jusqu'à ce jour, parce que ton oeuvre m'écrasait. A présent, je suis délivrée de la pierre et de l'art"[14] ("I could not return to you until today because your work was crushing me. Now, I am freed from stone and from art").

Again, Troyat's setting for the novella in a conventionally vague historical context, which may, incidentally, echo contemporary military events, allows him to introduce a supernatural event in a convincing manner. As in "Le Jugement de Dieu," he has created an authentic legend in which the miraculous is credible. At the same time, he has constructed the story on two new, interconnected themes: Lamansarde's removal from Catherine by his obsession, and the aesthetic nature of that *idée fixe*. Psychologically, the story offers a convincing description of the transformation of grief into obsessional activity and, finally, the worship of an object now far distant from the original love object. Lamansarde's battle with the Huguenots has nothing to do with Catherine's memory, but is concerned with the preservation of a fetish. Only when the fetish is destroyed can the original memory be revived. Yet, Lamansarde's obsession is specifically aesthetic in nature and, as such, offers a disquieting reflection upon the relationship between art and life. It is from art and stone that Catherine must be delivered, forces which contrast with the values of life and love. Troyat unequivocally conveys the implication that, because art is concerned with form and fixity, it acts ultimately as a barrier to the fluidity of existence. In this way "Le Puy Saint-Clair" condemns itself as a work of art and invites the reader to leave it for the complexity of life.

The third novella, "Le Merveilleux voyage de Jacques Mazeyrat" (The marvellous journey of Jacques Mazeyrat), is an exotic religious travel story which looks forward in tone and events to Claudel's *Le Soulier de satin*. Jacques Mazeyrat, a carpenter in the port of Dieppe, is seduced by the figurehead of a ship in the harbor and abandons his fiancée Véronique in order to sail with the vessel. In the course of his adventures, he loses the medallion representing St. John, given to him by Véronique, and the rest of the novella describes the way in which he retraces his steps in order to find it. Finally, the miraculous enters the novella: Mazeyrat discovers the medallion by chance and is brought home to Véronique by St. John himself.

In this story Troyat has used, more than in the two others, the material and structure of the folktale. Vladimir Propp, in *Morphology of the Folk-Tale*,[15] points out that ill-considered departures on the part of the hero, disastrous adventures, the loss of a talisman, followed by a miraculous restoration to the original location, are all firm elements of the fairy tale, and these are the sequences upon which Troyat's story is constructed. In this way, the very title, which emphasizes the marvellous and the format of the journey, announces the novella's place within a certain literary tradition. To these folktale elements of the plot structure, Troyat has added a Christian dimension which guarantees the magical powers of the talisman. More important, however, is the way in which the story follows on from its predecessor in denouncing human ambition in the form of art or travel, in the name of the couple and love. In both stories the natural relationship between the lovers is restored by divine intervention only after the pretensions of the hero to something wider have been exorcised. This cultivation of modest domesticity and human happiness was clearly a compelling value in France in 1941, but it connects also with the whole strain of antiambitious and antihistorical thinking embodied in Troyat's novels and *romans-fleuves*.

Le Jugement de Dieu is Troyat's last experiment with the novella form and it constitutes his only excursion into the genre of legend. In the particular circumstances of the Occupation, as he himself points out, such an excursion is eminently comprehensible. The legend, with its exotic, mythical past, is a welcome escape from the deprivations of German rule, and the supernatural rectification of destinies which have gone sadly wrong in the last two stories stands in stark contrast to the constant threat of arbitrary injustice. The legends also occupy a privileged position in the context of Troyat's whole work, momentarily transcending the psychological claustrophobia of the novels or the historical menace of the *romans-fleuves*. They stand in the same relation to Troyat's oeuvre as the ballets and the *Légende du roi Krogold*, in *Mort à crédit*, to Céline's whole production, an assertion of order and measure and escape in a context of decline and chaos. At the same time, they permit Troyat to experiment with a different stylistic register, that of the poetic fairy tale, through which he can create a new framework in which to evoke the fantastic. In this sense, the novellas become the pretext for a literary *tour de force* which does not necessarily open out unduly toward the real world.

Troyat has taken as a model Flaubert's "La Légende de Saint Julien l'Hospitalier," in which the stained-glass window at the end of the *conte* encloses the narrative in a purely aesthetic sphere and defines the preceeding narrative as the rich elaboration of a religious artifact. Nevertheless, Troyat is clearly disturbed by the implications of this model, and it is for this reason the "Le Puy Saint-Clair" implies a denunciation of exaggerated service to art and a plea for the normal and the humane. Even in the depths of the Occupation, and in the midst of his most satisfying escapist writing, Troyat refuses to concede his hard-won modest humanism.

Du Philanthrope à la Rouquine and *Le Geste d'Eve*

With *La Clef de voûte, La Fosse commune*, and *Le Jugement de Dieu*, Troyat has reached the full range of his explorations in the genres

of the novellas and the short story, moving from the exploitation
of the psychologically bizarre to the unambiguous world of the
supernatural, via the miraculous world of the legend. His two subsequent collections of short stories, *Du Philanthrope à la Rouquine*
(1945) and *Le Geste d'Eve* (1964), represent compilations of occasional
pieces with no overall architecture in either volume, and, by their
more sporadic appearance, testify to a difficulty in constantly renewing the genre, a fact which explains the absence of any further
collection after 1964.[16] Nevertheless, the two volumes mark a progression in Troyat's work by going further in their evocation of the
supernatural, an evocation which culminates in the appearance of
the Devil in *Le Geste d'Eve*.

Du Philanthrope à la Rouquine consists of nine stories—"Le Philanthrope," "Le Guéridon," "Le Portrait," "Le Fils du Ciel" (The
son of heaven), "La Gloire" (Glory), "Maldonne" (Mis-deal), "Le
Sortilège" (The spell), "La Verité" (Truth), and "La Rouquine"—
and takes its overall title from a combination of the first and last
stories. Like *La Fosse commune,* it proposes a range of subjects, from
the social comedy of "La Vérité," through the science fiction and
gentle political satire of "Le Philanthrope," to the stories in which
the supernatural dominates. Of these, the lightest is "Le Guéridon,"
which builds upon the theory explored in "Mr. Breadborough" that
the spirit world is merely a parallel to the world of human existence.
Its hero dies and discovers that the afterlife consists of the same
geographical features, populated by the whole community of the
dead, an image which, even more than in "Mr. Breadborough,"
prefigures the spirits of *Les Jeux sont faits.* Troyat's experiment with
the ghost story in "Le Ratuset" is continued in "Le Sortilège," in
which the narrator, again an army officer, reports a tale recounted
on a troop train at night. Once more, he is able to manipulate the
reader's responses by choosing a conventional but shifting setting
in which to situate the story-within-a-story, a case of apparent black
magic in a remote farm.

While the ghost story implies a safe return to normality, however,
other stories in the collection remain more disturbing, precisely
because they contrive to be open-ended. "Maldonne," for example,
raises the same question as that posed by "La Clef de voûte," whether
the narrator of an extreme experience is mad or whether that experience is genuinely inexplicable on rational terms. Dominique
Fauchois loses his wife Adèle, but grieves and prays so sincerely

that, like Catherine in "Le Puy Saint-Clair," she is returned to him. There all their troubles begin, however, and the miraculous gift is so rejected by the community that Fauchois is compelled to rectify the situation by murdering his wife and returning her to death. Equally disturbing is "Le Fils du Ciel," the ironic nickname of a *raté* who can only earn money by entering into a contract with a funeral director, Pilate, by which, on his own death, his wealthy brother will be enveigled into giving Pilate his custom. Full of remorse at every day which he spends in good health, "Le Fils du Ciel" decides to fulfill his part of the bargain by committing suicide, only to discover that Pilate has died before him. The apparent escape, however, is rendered more oblique by the hero's decision to approach a rival undertaker with the same proposition. Here, Troyat develops an ambiguity never totally resolved: it is not clear whether the desperate protagonist is merely exploiting a means of making money or whether , as a literal "Fils du Ciel," he has become an instrument of punishment for those who are the accomplices of death: "Mort celui qui s'était associé à la mort. Mort celui qui vivait de la mort. Pilate n'est plus que le client de Pilate"[17] ("The associate of death was dead. He who lived from death was dead. Pilate was no more than the client of Pilate").

Even more disturbing is "Le Portrait," in which Troyat uses supernatural ingredients to reinforce his anxiety at the relationship between the aesthetic mission of the artist and his life in the real world. Oscar Malvoisin arrives in a small town in the south of France and begins to paint portraits of the local gentry which reveal their souls rather than their physical appearance, thereby alienating most of the population. Eventually he marries and his portraits of his young beautiful bride show a vicious old woman. In the course of time, Malvoisin's wife becomes a saintly, beloved lady, and his final portrait encapsulates this by depicting her as a young girl. The supernatural element in the story, however, which plainly derives from Wilde's *Picture of Dorian Grey,* gives way to a more general problem: the intermediary of art prevents Malvoisin from experiencing the present value of his wife, either as a young girl or as a kind and mature being. Moreover, it is as if the artistic medium is a falsifying one: the representation of the old lady as a young girl is merely a cruel insult which encompasses none of the truth; the projection of the young girl into a vicious hag is denied by the subsequent development of Malvoisin's wife. The story becomes an important reflection on the barrier constituted by art and on its propensity to aim at aesthetically satisfying conclusions which bear little relation to fact.

Like *Du Philanhrope à la Rouquine, Le Geste d'Eve* comprises nine stories—"Les Mains" (The hands), "Le Carnet vert" (The green notebook), "Le Meilleur client" (The best client), "Le Retour de Versailles" (Return from Versailles), "Bouboule," "Vue imprenable" (Unrestricted view), "Faux Marbre" (False marble), "Le Diable emporte Pierre" (The devil takes away Pierre), and "Le Geste d'Eve" itself. These stories range from the bizarrely naturalistic to the supernatural: "Vue imprenable," for example, merely explores a situation totally explicable on rational terms. A lonely civil servant buys a country property only to find that it is being invaded by an alien presence. That presence is conclusively explained by the arrest of a half-witted tramp, but the protagonist realizes that so much of the attraction of the property is due to the intrusion, his only form of human contact, that without it the experience is valueless. Similarly, in a style reminiscent of René Clair's film *A Nous la liberté,* "Le Geste d'Eve" shows an industrialist forced to take the Metro because of a chauffeurs' strike falling under the spell of the ticket collector, Eve, and finding his life transformed temporarily as a result. In both cases, Troyat explores the psychology of isolation.

Similarly, "Le Carnet vert" may be interpreted on purely naturalistic lines: the hero finds a notebook, refuses newspaper advertisements to hand it back in the hope of a larger reward, only to find that it has been planted by an eccentric philanthropist anxious to reward honesty and that, with each day that passes, the reward diminishes. More whimsical is "Le Meilleur client," the tale of a florists' shop thrown into turmoil by a customer who orders the most extravagant selection of funeral wreaths. The worried owners discover that the customer is merely a lonely sick bachelor who wishes his funeral at least to give the lie to his solitude. Thus, in a significant proportion of the stories, Troyat explores the phenomenon of loneliness and concludes, in "Le Meilleur client," with an expression of human solidarity.

"Faux marbre" and "Bouboule" are only comprehensible with the reader's suspension of disbelief and his acceptance of the supernatural. The former continues Troyat's reflections on the problems of the aesthetic: the hero discovers the gift of painting objects so realistically that they appear to be made of marble. In a gesture of supreme logic, he finally paints himself and is transformed into a marble statue. Beneath the deftness of the story lies a familiar concern: the Midas-like quality of the artist who can produce aesthetic value only at the expense of isolation from existence.

"Bouboule" returns to the problem of isolation: le père Tabuze has as his only companion the dog Bouboule, who is taken from him by the interfering Madame de Montcaillou. On the way back from the veterinary surgeon's, however, the same phenomenon occurs as that which concludes "Le Tandem": Madame de Montcaillou's care is taken over by the ghost of Bouboule and she is wafted away into the afterlife.

These foundations of the supernatural are fully exploited in two final stories in which a satanic presence is revealed. "Le Diable emporte Pierre" treats the subject in jocular manner, using the form of the folktale to recount a village practical joke which backfires. The Devil, who is supposed to carry away the village idiot, Pierre, instead bears off the instigator of the plot. Yet Troyat's richest working of the genre occurs in "Le Retour de Versailles," in which a young couple, Georges and Caroline, buy a fifteenth-century Flemish painting at an auction in Versailles against stiff competition from a remarkable old couple. Georges gets up to clean the painting at night and is found dead the next morning, with a cleaned part of the picture revealing the sinister old couple at the mouth of Hell. The story relies for its effect upon its ambiguity: either Georges is supernaturally punished for preventing the reunification of the couple with their painting or he is the chosen figure for their return from limbo to the fixed pose at the Gates of Hell. In other words, is the cleaning of the damaged part of the painting merely an act of fatal revelation of a literal act of restoration, permitting the transfer of the two spirits and destroying the intermediary in the process? It is this uncertainty and speculation which constitutes the richness of the story, a richness to which the progression of the short stories as a whole tends, from *La Fosse commune,* through *Du Philanthrope à la Rouquine,* to *Le Geste d'Eve.*

The Strange, the Marvellous, and the Fantastic

The difficulty experienced by the reader in "Le Retour de Versailles" is one which is common to a large number of Troyat's short stories and which helps to situate them in the genre of "littérature fantastique." In his essay on the subject, Tzvetan Todorov defines the fantastic in literature by the hesitation felt by the implicit reader at a series of events which are susceptible of either a naturalistic or a supernatural interpretation: "Le fantastique, c'est l'hésitation éprouvée par un être qui ne connaît que les lois naturelles, face à un événement en apparence surnaturel"[18] ("The fantastic is the hesitation experienced by someone who knows only natural laws when confronted with an apparently supernatural event"). The key term in this definition is "en apparence," for it introduces the distrust of the reader for the apparently unreal and his attempts to explain supernatural phenomena in terms of external artifice or the workings of the imagination. From this initial hypothesis, Todorov is able to arrive at a full categorization of the fantastic which embraces the reader, the style, and the theme: three conditions are necessary:

"D'abord, il faut que le texte oblige le lecteur à considérer le monde des personnages comme un monde de personnes vivantes et à hésiter entre une explication naturelle et une explication surnaturelle des événements évoqués. Ensuite, cette hésitation peut être ressentie également par un personnage; ainsi le rôle de lecteur est pour ainsi dire confié à un personnage et dans le même temps l'hésitation se trouve représentée, elle devient un des thèmes de l'oeuvre. . . . Enfin, il importe que le lecteur adopte une certaine attitude à l'égard du texte: il refusera aussi bien l'interprétation allégorique que l'interprétation "poétique".[19]

First, the text must oblige the reader to consider the world of the characters as a world of real people and to hesitate between a natural and a supernatural explanation for the events recounted. Then, this hesitation may be felt by a character; thus, the role of the reader is, so to speak, given to a character and, at the same time, the hesitation becomes represented, it becomes one of the themes. . . . Finally, it is vital that the reader adopt a certain attitude toward the text, that he refuse both an allegorical or "poetic" interpretation.

With this precise definition, Todorov is able to distinguish the properly fantastic from similar but fundamentally different genres: poetic and allegorical writing, and the separate genres of "l'étrange" and "le merveilleux."

Both of these genres avoid the hesitation essential to the fantastic: "l'étrange" is concerned with a series of bizarre events with a rational explanation; at the other pole, "le merveilleux" evokes happenings whose supernatural qualities are never doubted. Where these genres coincide with the fantastic is in the endings of the narrative: the "fantastique-étrange" will resolve the reader's doubt by a logical naturalistic explanation; the "fantastique-merveilleux" resolves that doubt by introducing an incontrovertibly supernatural final cause. These categories established by Todorov are of undoubted assistance in classifying Troyat's short stories and novellas. *Le Jugement de Dieu,* for example, stands at the head of a series of tales in which the supernatural motive power can never be questioned. The very title of "Le Merveilleux voyage de Jacques Mazeyrat" serves to underline the connection between the marvellous and supernatural intervention, a connection which applies equally to "diabolical" stories, such as "Le Tandem" and "Bouboule," and to the spiritualist and science-fiction tales, "Mr. Breadborough," "Les Cobayes," "Le Guéridon," and "Le Philanthrope." In none of these pieces is the reader placed in a state of hesitation regarding the status of the events evoked. Similarly, the thread of stories beginning with "Monsieur Citrine" and concluding with "Le Carnet vert" is concerned with the genre of the strange, relying upon the psychologically abnormal or the incongruous juxtaposition of events and, again, abolishes the crucial element of doubt.

"La Clef de voûte," however, is a different matter. It has a first-person narrator who is puzzled at his own fate and so introduces the puzzlement as a theme. It then places the narrator and the reader before a choice in interpretation: whether the shadow/ghost of the dead sister is real, to be taken literally, or whether it is a symptom of an acute psychological state stemming from the relationship with Thérèse and guilt at her death. Classic examples of this type of writing are found in the conventions of the ghost story: the ambiguous interpretation of events in "Le Ratuset" and "Le Sortilège." If these examples show the affinities between the fantastic and the strange, "L'Ame de Mélitone" demonstrates the connection with the marvellous and the distance from it. It describes a young boy Serge, who goes out on Christmas night in order to save the soul of the gamekeeper Mélitone by bringing him to church. The child gets lost in a blizzard, is found by chance by Mélitone who takes him to the nearest habitation, which turns out to be the packed church at Christmas mass. The story can be read in two ways: either the rescue of Serge is pure coincidence, with pleasing overtones, or it is a Christmas miracle. What keeps the tale in the realm of the fantastic, however, is the way in which the reader is maintained between the two interpretations where absolute explanations do not apply.

Bracketed on one side by the tales which are merely bizarre and on the other by miracles like "Mélitone," the genuinely fantastic stories of Troyat combine a greater textual activity and abstract speculation with a profound psychological exploration in the way that the fantastic has its origins in the narrator's unconscious. Nevertheless, Todorov is rigorous in his definition of fantastic literature as a short-lived genre, running from the late eighteenth century to the end of the nineteenth. Rather too dismissively, he rejects any claim by twentieth-century writing to be fantastic, basing his argument on the vital element of plot in the fantastic tale, a nineteenth-century phenomenon which gives way to increased textual self-reflexiveness in modern writing. At the same time, he argues more convincingly that any concept of the fantastic must be based upon a firm acceptance of the real, a concept which, in the era of relativity, has less weight. This global view has the effect of facilitating an integration of Troyat's short stories into his entire output.

As a novelist, Troyat has used fundamentally traditional models and has attempted to maintain a realist tradition. In other words, the real is an essential component of Troyat's novels and *romans-fleuves* in which the principle is reinforced by historically verifiable detail and footnotes. Within the context of Troyat's work as a whole, therefore, the short stories play a vital role in reacting against and extending the concept of the real and in dealing with themes and situations unacceptable in the world of realist fiction. The short stories, therefore, are less of an anomaly in Troyat's work than they at first sight seem: they reinforce his role as a traditionalist, but also react against the constraints of reality represented most obviously by the biographies but also by the other fiction, to produce some of the finest examples of his writing.

Chapter Six
Conclusion

We are now in a position to see how Troyat, as a realist writer, operates with different levels of reality in his prose. The fantastic and bizarre short stories, far from constituting a radical break with the work of the realist novelist, feed upon that work and use it as an indispensable point of departure for a world of fictional experiment. At the other extreme are the unsatisfactory works of reportage—*La Case de l'Oncle Sam, De Gratte-ciel en cocotier,* and *La Naissance d'une Dauphine*—in which the immediate presence of the reality is an embarrassment demanding the mediation of the "ton amusé." Between these two extremities lie the short novels, with their detached evocation, and analysis of psychological tension, the *romans-fleuves,* with their cold view of the process of history, and the biographies.

This study has contained no extended formal analysis of the biographies of Dostoevski (1940), Pushkin (1946), Lermontov (1952), Tolstoy (1965), Gogol (1971), Catherine the Great (1977), Peter the Great (1979), Alexander 1st (1981), and Ivan the Terrible (1982), for the reason that no satisfactory methodology exists for discussing biography, as opposed to autobiography, and that such analysis is inevitably thrown back on to discussion of the subject rather than the treatment. Nevertheless, they constitute a body of work which, possibly more than the prose fiction, will guarantee Troyat's place in French literary history. In spite of being tempted by a biography of Flaubert, he has restricted himself to Russian subjects, arguing that his knowledge of the language places him in a privileged position to communicate original information to his French audience. The works are scrupulously documented, mainly from Russian sources, and therefore constitute serious attempts to manipulate data in order to understand an external subject. In this respect, Troyat reveals himself once more a traditionalist, employing the omniscience of the classic nineteenth-century biographer and refusing to adopt the partisan stance of Romain Rolland's *Tolstoï* (1911), the "biographie romancée" of André Maurois's *Prométhée* (1965) or *Ariel* (1923), or the psychoanalytical re-creation of Flaubert in Sartre's *L'Idiot de la famille* (1971–72). At the same time, Troyat's biographies demonstrate his economical exploitation of his resources: it has already been seen how *Grimbosq* lays the foundations for *Pierre le Grand,* as does, conversely, *Catherine la Grande* for *Le Prisonnier No. 1.* Yet this is a relationship between different biographies and between biography and *roman-fleuve* which exists from 1940 onward. *L'Etrange destin de Lermontov* (The strange destiny of Lermontov) is born directly from *Pouchkine;* Dostoevski himself appears in *Sophie ou la fin des combats;* the material for the biographies of Pushkin and Lermontov primes the first three volumes of *La Lumière des justes.*

Finally, in his choice of subjects, Troyat has once more demonstrated his need to maintain a distance between himself and his work. In this respect, it is the omissions which are the most significant: there is no study of Turgenev, who, as a realist writer, has strong affinities with Troyat, nor of Chekhov, an author to whom the biographer feels so close that writing becomes impossible.

Troyat's immense literary production has brought him both public recognition and commercial success. It remains to be seen whether that immediate success will be transformed into lasting critical recognition. Two barriers to that will undoubtedly be his role as a traditionalist and a best-seller. The traditionalism need not, of course, constitute a barrier: for the most part, Troyat's use of the ultratraditional form of the *roman-fleuve* is productive, and his work within the genre of biography is one of his most successful achievements. The problem is most acute in the short novels, in which the format of the brief realist analysis does not enable the full force of the subject to be developed. Inevitably, this problem is compounded by that of commercialism: the short novels after the war tend to repeat a series of formulas which have proved successful without, on the whole, exploring new ground thematically or developing structurally. This becomes most serious in the last two volumes of *Les Semailles et les moissons,* in which the authentic analyses of the first three volumes give way to commercial stereotypes. Similarly, *Le Moscovite* is ruled by its plot and its exotic historical setting rather than by any serious thematic concern. To a large extent, these dangers are endemic to Troyat's original ambition, to be a "storyteller and creator of myths." The storyteller is inescapably in the marketplace and runs the risk of commercialism. Yet the stories themselves have their own value, a value enhanced when they become myth, when they take on larger preoccupations. On one level, Troyat remains important as a highly competent literary craftsman in an age of fictional ostentation. But the works which attain a different dimension are those, like the short stories, which allow a constraint of reality to be relaxed, or the *romans-fleuves*, in which abstract concerns are finally voiced—the domination and ultimate futility of history, mitigated by a modest faith in the fleeting moments of human happiness.

Notes and References

Chapter One

1. *Un si long chemin* (Paris, 1976), p. 237.
2. In the final volume of *Les Semailles et les moissons,* Troyat shows how this delusion reached such a point that Hitler's invasion of Russia in 1941 was hailed as a war of liberation which would permit the exiles to return home.
3. *Un si long chemin,* p. 39.
4. A point made clearly in *Sainte Russie: Souvenirs et réflexions.*
5. In *Un si long chemin,* p. 61, Troyat recalls the feeling of shock and guilt among the Russian community at the assassination of President Paul Doumer by a Russian in 1932.
6. Who serves as the basis for Guillaume, in *Faux Jour.*
7. Volodia Bylinine recurs in Troyat's career in connection with *Le Mort saisit le vif.*
8. *Un si long chemin,* p. 50.
9. Ibid., p. 56.
10. Marcel Arland, "Essais critiques," *Nouvelle Revue Française* 303 (1938):1045.
11. *Un si long chemin,* p. 51.
12. Ibid., p. 71.
13. Ibid., p. 91.
14. Ibid., p. 94.
15. Ibid., p. 169.
16. Gilbert Ganne, *Messieurs les best-sellers* (Paris: Perrin, 1966).
17. By coincidence, it was Farrère who was with Paul Doumer when he was assassinated and who tried to save the President.
18. *Un si long chemin,* p. 240.
19. Maurice Chavardès, in *Un si long chemin,* p. 8.
20. R.-M. Albérès, *Le Roman d'aujourd'hui 1960–1970* (Paris, 1970).
21. Reported in André Breton, *Manifestes du surréalisme* (Paris: Jean-Jacques Pauvert, 1972), p. 19.
22. *Un si long chemin,* pp. 242–43.
23. Ibid., p. 239.
24. See, for example, Shestov's *La Philosophie de la tragédie* (Paris: Schiffrin, 1926).

25. See *Un si long chemin,* p. 97.

26. Ibid., p. 256.

27. Ibid., p. 192.

28. Jean Ricardou, *Problèmes du nouveau roman* (Paris: Seuil, 1967), p. 111.

29. Raymond Queneau, "Technique du roman," in *Bâtons, chiffres et lettres* (Paris: Gallimard, 1950).

30. *La Case de l'oncle Sam* (Paris, 1960), p. 169.

31. See *Un si long chemin,* p. 73.

32. Ganne, *Messieurs les best-sellers,* p. 36.

Chapter Two

1. See Pierre de Boisdeffre, *Une Histoire vivante de la littérature d'aujourd'hui* (Paris, 1962); Albérès, *Le Roman d'aujourd'hui 1960–1970;* Louis Chaigne, *Les Lettres contemporaines* (Paris, 1964).

2. J. S. Wood, Introduction to *La Tête sur les épaules* (London, 1961), p. 11.

3. Jean Vaudal, *"Faux Jour,* par Henri Troyat," *Nouvelle Revue Française* 259 (1935):626.

4. Henri Troyat, *Faux Jour* (Paris, 1952), p. 8.

5. Vaudal, *"Faux-Jour,* par Henri Troyat," p. 625–26.

6. L.-F. Céline, *Guignol's Band* (Paris: Gallimard, 1972), p. 377.

7. Jean Vaudal, *"Le Vivier,* par Henri Troyat," *Nouvelle Revue Française,* 267 (1935):934.

8. Ibid., pp. 934–35.

9. *Un si long chemin,* p. 68.

10. *Le Vivier,* (Paris, 1959), p. 18.

11. Vaudal, *"Le Vivier,* par Henri Troyat," p. 934.

12. *L'Araigne* (Paris, 1938).

13. Arland, "Essais critiques," p. 1045.

14. Ibid., p. 1046.'

15. Ibid.

16. In conversation with the author.

17. *Judith Madrier* (Paris, 1940), p. 9.

18. *Un si long chemin,* p. 96.

19. *Le Mort saisit le vif* (Paris, 1942), p. 92.

20. See Jean-Paul Sartre, *L'Etre et le néant* (Paris: Gallimard, 1943), p. 98.

21. *Le Signe du taureau* (Paris, 1977).

22. Jean Giraudoux, *Intermezzo* (Paris: Grasset, 1933), p. 118.

23. Significantly, one of the members of the jury who views Gèvres's statue is called Pasquier.

24. Arland, "Essais critiques," p. 1046.

Chapter Three

1. See *Un si long chemin,* pp. 140–41.
2. J. S. Wood, Introduction to *La Tête sur les épaules,* p. 25.
3. Ibid., p. 25.
4. Francis Jeanson, *Sartre par lui-même* (Paris: Seuil, 1955), p. 129.
5. Jean-Paul Sartre, *L'Existentialisme est un humanisme* (Paris: Nagel, 1946), pp. 39–40.
6. For Troyat's own reaction to the film version of his novel, see *Un si long chemin,* pp. 149–150.
7. See ibid., pp. 146–47.
8. Quoted in W. D. Howarth, Introduction to *La Neige en deuil* (London: 1954), pp. 11–12.
9. Ibid., p. 11.
10. Ganne, *Messieurs les best-sellers,* p. 114.
11. *Une Extrême amitié* (Paris, 1967), p. 46.
12. *La Pierre, la feuille et les ciseaux* (Paris, 1972), pp. 128–29.
13. *Anne Prédaille* (Paris, 1973), p. 58.
14. *Grimbosq* (Paris, 1976), p. 208.
15. *Le Prisonnier No. 1* (Paris, 1978), p. 13.
16. *Viou* (Paris, 1980), p. 49.

Chapter Four

1. *Etrangers sur la terre,* (Paris, 1972), 2:440.
2. See *Un si long chemin,* p. 105.
3. See ibid., p. 102.
4. Genesis, 8:22.
5. See *Un si long chemin,* pp. 153–61.
6. It is interesting that the melodramatization of Christian indicates Troyat's anxiety at his cynical amoralism.
7. André Malraux, *L'Espoir,* in *Romans* (Paris: Gallimard, 1947), p. 851.
8. *Sophie ou la fin des combats* (Paris, 1963), p. 11.
9. *La Barynia* (Paris, 1967), p. 135.
10. *Les Dames de Sibérie* (Paris, 1962), p. 204.
11. *La Barynia,* p. 240, paraphrasing Proverbs 13:9.
12. *Sophie, ou la fin des combats,* p. 23.
13. *La Faim des lionceaux* (Paris, 1966), p. 324.
14. *Le Cahier* (Paris, 1968), p. 261.
15. *Le Moscovite* (Paris, 1974), p. 173.
16. *La Vie quotidienne en Russie au temps du dernier Tsar* (Paris, 1959), p. 5.

Chapter Five

1. Marcel Arland, "Chronique des romans," *Nouvelle Revue Française* 280 (1937):157.

2. See ibid.

3. Ibid.

4. Ibid.

5. A further collection, *Les Ailes du Diable,* published in 1966, is a selection of work from the previous volumes and not a separate work in its own right. In addition, there are isolated works, such as *La Maison des bêtes heureuses* and "L'Ame de Mélitone," both of 1956.

6. For a full discussion of the French short story in the twentieth century, see René Godenne, "La Nouvelle Française au XXe siècle," *Europe,* August–September 1981.

7. *La Clef de voûte* (Paris, 1937), p. 23.

8. Arland, "Chronique des romans," p. 157.

9. Ibid.

10. *La Fosse commune* (Paris, 1974), pp. 130–31.

11. The gap between subjective and objective interpretations of experience is of course fully explored in Camus's *L'Etranger.*

12. *Les Ailes du Diable* (Paris, 1966), p. 235.

13. See *Un si long chemin,* p. 96.

14. *Le Jugement de Dieu* (Paris, 1941), p. 164.

15. Vladimir Propp, *Morphology of the Folk-tale* (Austin: University of Texas Press, 1968).

16. A fact confirmed in conversation with the author.

17. *Les Ailes du Diable,* p. 60.

18. Tzvetan Todorov, *Introduction à la littérature fantastique,* (Paris: Seuil, 1970), p. 29.

19. Ibid., pp. 37–38.

Selected Bibliography

PRIMARY SOURCES

1. Novels
Faux Jour. Paris: Plon, 1935.
Le Vivier. Paris: Plon, 1935.
Grandeur Nature. Paris: Plon, 1936.
L'Araigne, Paris: Plon, 1938.
Judith Madrier. Paris: Plon, 1940.
Le Mort saisit le vif. Paris: Plon, 1942.
Le Signe du taureau. Paris: Plon, 1945.
La Tête sur les épaules. Paris: Plon, 1951.
La Neige en deuil. Paris: Flammarion, 1952.
Une Extrême amitié. Paris: Editions de la Table Ronde, 1963.
La Pierre, la feuille et les ciseaux. Paris: Flammarion, 1972.
Anne Prédaille. Paris: Flammarion, 1973.
Grimbosq. Paris: Flammarion, 1976.
Le Front dans les nuages. Paris: Flammarion, 1977.
Le Prisonnier No. 1. Paris: Flammarion, 1978.
Viou. Paris: Flammarion, 1980.
Le Pain de l'étranger. Paris: Flammarion, 1981.

2. Novel cycles
Tant que la terre durera. Paris: Editions de la Table Ronde, 1947–50. *Tant que la terre durera* (1947); *Le Sac et la cendre* (1948); *Etrangers sur la terre* (1950).
Les Semailles et les moissons. Paris: Plon, 1953–58. *Les Semailles et les moissons* (1953); *Amélie* (1955); *La Grive* (1956); *Tendre et violente Elizabeth* (1957); *La Rencontre* (1958).
La Lumière des justes. Paris: Flammarion, 1959–63. *Les Compagnons du coquelicot* (1959); *La Barynia* (1959); *La Gloire des vaincus* (1961); *Les Dames de Sibérie* (1962); *Sophie ou la fin des combats* (1963).
Les Eygletière. Paris: Flammarion, 1965–67. *Les Eygletière* (1965); *La Faim des lionceaux* (1966); *La Malandre* (1967).
Les Héritiers de l'avenir. Paris: Flammarion, 1968–70. *Le Cahier* (1968); *Cent un coups de canon* (1969); *L'Eléphant blanc* (1970).

Le Moscovite. Paris: Flammarion, 1974–76. *Le Moscovite* (1974); *Les Désordres secrets* (1975); *Les Feux du matin* (1976).

3. Short stories and novellas
La Clef de voûte. Paris: Plon, 1937.
La Fosse commune. Paris: Plon, 1939.
Le Jugement de Dieu. Paris: Plon, 1941.
Du Philanthrope à la Rouquine. Paris: Plon, 1945.
La Maison des bêtes heureuses. Paris: Bias, 1956.
"L'Ame de Mélitone." In *Contes des pays de neige,* by Arthur Ransome et al. Paris: Flammarion, 1956.
Le Geste d'Eve. Paris: Flammarion, 1964.
Les Ailes du Diable. Paris: Flammarion, 1966.

4. Biography and nonfiction
"Dostoievski le joueur." *Oeuvres Libres* 219 (September 1939).
Dostoievski. Paris: Fayard, 1940.
Les Ponts de Paris, Aquarelles de René Kuder. Paris: Flammarion, 1946.
Pouchkine. Paris: Albin Michel, 1946.
"Lettre de Paris, le 27 juin 1946." *Nouvelles Epîtres,* 34 (1947).
"Preface." *Manon Lescaut,* by l'abbé Prévost, Paris: Fayard, 1947.
La Case de l'Oncle Sam. Paris: Editions de la Table Ronde, 1948.
L'Etrange destin de Lermontov. Paris: Plon, 1952.
"Alexandre Sergéevitch Pouchkine, 1799–1835." In *Oeuvres complètes,* by Pushkin. Vol. 1. Paris: André Bonne, 1953.
De Gratte-ciel en cocottier: A travers l'Amérique indienne. Paris: Plon, 1955.
"Vie, martyre et gloire de Dostoievski." In *L'Eternel mari,* by Dostoevski. Paris: Editions de la Bibliothèque Mondiale, 1956.
Sainte Russie: Souvenirs et réflexions. Paris: Grasset, 1956.
La Vie quotidienne en Russie au temps du dernier tsar. Paris: Hachette, 1959.
Naissance d'une Dauphine. Paris: Gallimard, 1960.
Discours de réception à l'Académie Française. Paris: Plon, 1960.
Tolstoï. Paris: Faynard, 1965.
Gogol. Paris: Flammarion, 1971.
Un si long chemin: Conversations avec Maurice Chavardès. Paris: Stock, 1976.
Catherine la Grande. Paris: Flammarion, 1977.
Pierre le Grand. Paris: Flammarion, 1979.
Alexandre Ier, le Sphinx du Nord. Paris: Flammarion, 1981.
Ivan le terrible. Paris: Flammarion, 1982.

5. Plays
Les Vivants. Paris: André Bonne, 1946.
Sébastien. *Opéra: Supplément Théâtral* 4 (1949).

L'Assassinat d'Alexandre II. Pièce radiophonique. In *Sainte Russie: Souvenirs et réflexions.* Paris: Grasset, 1956.

6. English Translations

One Minus Two. New York: Washburn, 1938. Translation of *Grandeur Nature.*

Judith Madrier. New York: Washburn, 1941.

Firebrand: the Life of Dostoievsky. New York: Roy, 1946.

Pushkin: A Biography. New York: Pantheon, 1950.

My Father's House. New York: Duell, Sloan and Pearce, 1951; *Sackcloth and Ashes.* London: Arco, 1956; *Strangers in the Land.* New York: Crowell, 1956. Translation of [the trilogy *Tant que la terre durera*].

The Mountain. New York: Simon and Schuster, 1953.Translation of *La Neige en deuil.*

Amélie in love. New York: Simon and Schuster, 1956; *Amélie and Pierre.* New York: Simon and Schuster, 1957; *Elizabeth. A Novel.* New York: Simon and Schuster, 1959; *Tender and Violent Elizabeth.* New York: Simon and Schuster, 1961; *The Encounter.* New York: Simon and Schuster, 1962. Translation of *Les Semailles et les moissons.*

The Brotherhood of the Red Poppy. New York: Simon and Schuster, 1961; *The Baroness.* New York: Simon and Schuster, 1961. Translation of *La Lumière des justes.*

Daily Life in Russia under the Last Tsar. New York: Macmillan, 1962.

Tolstoy, London: Allen, 1968.

Gogol, the Biography of a Divided Soul. London: Allen and Unwin, 1974.

Head in the Clouds. Henley-on-Thames: Ellis, 1979. Translation of *Le Front dans les nuages.*

Catherine the Great. Henley-on-Thames: Ellis, 1979.

Viou. Henley-on-Thames: Ellis, 1981.

SECONDARY SOURCES

Alberes, R.-M., "Saveurs de la chronique." in *Le Roman d'aujourd'hui 1960–1970.* Paris: Albin Michel, 1970, pp. 9–15. Enthusiastic study of Troyat in the context of the postwar *roman-fleuve.*

Boak, Denis. "Henri Troyat." In *Critical Bibliography of French Literature.* Vol. 6 *Twentieth Century,* vol. 3. Syracuse: University of Syracuse Press, 1980, p. 1751. Useful guide to secondary material.

Boisdeffre, Pierre de. "Romans-cycles." In *Une Histoire vivante de la littérature d'aujourd'hui 1939–1961.* Paris: Perrin, 1962, pp. 266–267. Brief discussion of Troyat's *romans-fleuves.*

Chaigne, Louis. "Le Roman." In *Les Lettres contemporains*. Paris: Del Duca, 1964, pp. 577–79. Discussion of Troyat's *romans-fleuves*.

Hewitt, Nicholas. Introduction to *Grandeur Nature*. London: Methuen, 1980. Analysis of the novel in the context of Troyat's short fiction.

Howarth, W. D. Introduction to *La Neige en deuil*. London: Harrap, 1954. Useful detailed analysis of the novel.

Lehner, Frederick. "Henri Troyat." *French Review* 17 (January 1944): 149–53. Shows Troyat's debt to Dostoievsky in his novels.

Nathan, Jacques. "La Fin de l'après-guerre." In *Histoire de la littérature contemporaine*. Paris: L'Activité Contemporaine, 1954, pp. 286–89. Discussion of the *romans-fleuves*.

Tahan, Ilana Antoinette. "The Novels of Henri Troyat." M.Phil. thesis, University of Aston, Birmingham, England, 1976. General discussion and exposition of Troyat's short novels and *romans-fleuves*.

Wood, J. S. Introduction to *La Tête sur les épaules*. London: University of London Press, 1961. Interesting detailed analysis of the novel, though exaggerated in claims for Troyat's status in general.

Index